CONTENTS

INTRODUCTION

Running a pet hotel for cats and dogs was a new career move for Geoff and he describes how the idea came about. The premises are set in the beautiful county of Shropshire in the very heart of rural England.

Geoff enlightens readers about unpredictable events and scenarios that are humorous, factual and even traumatic. His unique stories are diversified and are not just about cats and dogs. For example, Geoff encounters a very rare endangered species in Thailand.

Introducing each chapter is an outstanding caricature giving a visual clue to the next extraordinary chain of events.

Many a pet lover's dream is to own and run a pet hotel for cats and dogs, but after reading Geoff's long-kept secrets, they might well have second

thoughts...

Please study Home Sweet Home because a lot of the action took place here, and when I say action...

I mean... ACTION!!!

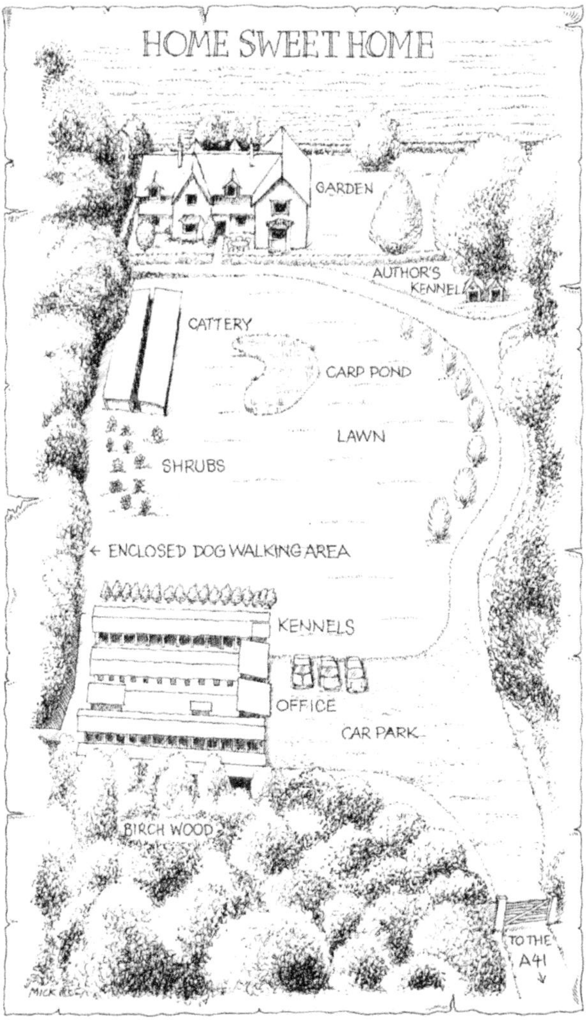

CHAPTER 1

How a Simple Conversation Can Completely Change One's Life

MICK

Now here is how the pet hotel started. And how the saying, 'Being in the right place at the right time', can ring so true.

Before we started the pet hotel, my wife Kathy and I lived in the picturesque one-hundred-and-fifty-year old sandstone cottage, known as Keepers Cottage. Originally, the cottage housed a long line of gamekeepers and belonged to Chetwynd Estate. (I was the last gamekeeper to reside there.) Keepers Cottage was situated just three miles north of the market town of Newport, Shropshire England where I was born. Eventually, Keepers Cottage became the home of our pet boarding business.

When I worked from the cottage as a self-employed gamekeeper, I was in charge of more than two thousand acres of arable farm and woodland in the surrounding area. And for sure, if I had my life again, I would include those nine glorious years working so close to nature. As much as I enjoyed the job, the gamekeeping bug was coming out of me and it was time to move on and start a new career.

Kathy had a secure managerial career with

Barclays Bank in her home county of Cheshire, which was a fifty-mile drive away.

But what did my future hold?

Before my gamekeeping career took off, I was a self-employed salesman making big money and driving more than one thousand miles a week. I enjoyed the driving but hated the selling and I most certainly did not want to go back to that if I could help it.

So, day after day, we racked our brains.

As luck would have it, in my final year as a gamekeeper the owner of Chetwynd Estate died. The Estate was split up and sold off. So we were incredibly fortunate to be 'In the right place at the right time' and able to buy our dream cottage.

But after our incredibly good fortune, I was still in need of work.

Because I was the local gamekeeper all the farmers knew me, therefore I was free to roam anywhere in the surrounding countryside with Sally my Springer Spaniel.

How lucky is that?

One day that I will never forget, Sally and I walked to the nearby woodland called Shutts

Wood. Sally was walking to heel when I heard the rasping sound of a chainsaw. I knew it belonged to Dave the woodman. With me being the gamekeeper, I always took the chance to talk to woodmen because they are very observant people and it is incredible how much information one can glean from them.

Dave was busy logging a dead oak tree that had fallen in a storm the previous winter. With chainsaws being dangerous machines, Sally and I approached him from the front. He acknowledged me and cut the engine and I welcomed the silence.

We struck up a pleasant conversation about my favourite subject, nature.

The conversation moved away from trees, pheasants, foxes, badgers and country life to holidays. I heard that Dave had just been on holiday to Cornwall. I knew he owned two German Shepherds and I was interested to know who had taken care of them when he was away.

So, I asked,

"Dave, when you were in Cornwall, who looked after your dogs?"

He replied,

“I took them to a boarding kennel and it cost me an arm and a leg.”

Getting interested, I said,

“How much was it Dave?”

"Forty-five quid!"

I was astounded,

“Jesus, they must be raking it in!”

Our conversation was taking place on the edge of Shutts Wood which was on a bit of a hill, and five hundred yards below us standing in all its glory was Keepers Cottage.

Dave gave me a knowing look and said,

“I can hear your brain working. Are you thinking what I’m thinking?”

I replied,

“I’ve been way, way in front of you for the last few minutes mate.”

Dave replied,

"You've got big pound signs in your eyes. They're rolling like one-armed bandits."

So, on that very memorable day, the idea of a hotel for cats and dogs was born.

On my walk back to Keepers Cottage I was so excited. My mind was racing at a hundred miles an hour.

'Where do we go from here? How do we start this project?'

I couldn't wait for Kathy to arrive home from work so that I could discuss my fantastic new idea. The idea of a hotel for cats and dogs sounded right up my street. I had enjoyed training gundogs, and now I had a chance to work with dogs again. As a bonus, I was going to get paid for it as well!

And yes, what about cats? My mind was in a whirl. I had already made my first million before Kathy had started her long journey from Cheshire. My brain was in overdrive. At 7 p.m. when I heard Kathy's car pulling up outside, I couldn't wait to open the front door.

I swung the front door wide open and with a big smile on my face proudly proclaimed,

"Geoff's got a new career!"

Kathy with a puzzled look on her face said,

"Doing what?"

"I'm going to open a hotel for cats and dogs."

She beamed, with her beautiful 'Cheshire smile' and said,

"Where on earth did that idea come from?

I replied,

"I was talking to Dave the woodman up at Shutts Wood. He told me he had been charged forty-five quid for his two German Shepherds at a boarding kennel in Newport."

Kathy was astounded and said,

"That's one heck of a lot of money. What a brilliant idea for you."

So, there you have it, a massive change in my life. My new career was about to begin.

All night long we discussed how we should go about it. My brain was racing away with anticipation.

I said to Kathy,

"It won't take me long to knock up some kennels, runs and cat cages with a bit of wood, wire and concrete."

BUT, LITTLE DID I KNOW, IT WASN'T GOING TO BE THAT SIMPLE.

After hours of planning, we decided we needed to do a lot of research for the new exciting idea. It has always been my opinion that if a job needs doing, it needs doing correctly. The first thing we did was to look up pet hotels/catteries and kennels in the local Yellow Pages...

But it was bad news!

We were shocked...

Because there were dozens of them.

In fact, there were over seventy of them. With there being so many, it made us feel really disappointed and even worse, discouraged.

'How on earth can we make a living out of this if we have so much competition?'

Not being the type of people who give up easily,

the following weekend trying not to be too downhearted, we decided to look at some of the future opposition's facilities that were advertised in Yellow Pages.

Enter, '*Geoff Bond 008*', the new spy on the block and his pretty blonde accomplice, Kathy.

So, this is when we entered the world of industrial espionage!

We visited several pet boarding establishments in the surrounding area relishing our new spying profession by pretending that we had a cat and dog to board.

What cat? We didn't even own one.

As we toured the county, we were amazed and sometimes shocked by what we saw.

The standards in virtually all of the boarding establishments were generally poor. A lot of the buildings were ancient, dirty and draughty. In some cases, the runs for the dogs were so small that large dogs could only turn around if they got up onto their hind legs. Some dogs had no choice but to sit in their excrement. And their stressful barking was horrendous. Also, cats were sleeping in the same buildings as noisy dogs, and most people do not realise that cats' hearing is far more sensitive than humans. Unfortunately, the stressed-out cats could not put their paws over their ears to block out the relentless noise.

My words to Kathy were,

“Most of these places are not fit to house a pig!”

We met proprietors who were running their businesses single-handed. One lady said she was really struggling to cope and had already suffered two nervous breakdowns.

‘What? Nervous breakdowns!!!’

I was more than a tad worried about this startling information, especially coming from the tranquillity of game-keeping. The last thing I needed in my life was a N-N-N-N-Nervous breakdown.

Anyway, the good news was, after a few weekends of this type of spying, sorry research, we concluded that only a few establishments could give us any serious opposition.

By then, we had made up our minds...

It was, ‘Game On’!

Gone, was my idea of building our new facilities with cheap wood and wire.

We needed bricks, mortar and steel!

I was going to create a palace fit for a King and Queen.

Or even cats and dogs.

I was quite determined that we were going to have five-star facilities.

As far as I was concerned, ours was going to be the best pet hotel in the UK.

CHAPTER 2

Obeying Strict Rules and Regulations

Chapters two and three are about getting started and could be of interest to some of you who would like to know the stages (trials and tribulations) we had to go through to get our pet hotel off the ground. Maybe you would like a pet hotel of your own.

After chapter three, as in the earlier books of this series, the animal stories start to flow.

It wasn't too long before I found out that an establishment for cats and dogs required planning permission and to my dismay that approval from the authorities is not guaranteed. Indeed, there are worrying conditions to fulfil.

Initially, I needed a professional architect to draw up plans from my own not-so-professional designs and drawings. Finding an architect was no problem. I just got out the good old Yellow Pages and within a short period, we had professional plans to submit to the Council for approval.

With my research, I found out there were two main requirements.

Number 1 - Noise Level

Noise could be a possible nuisance factor in the surrounding area. Let's face it, a whole building full of dogs could make quite a row. Noise can travel a long way, especially carried by the wind and noise of any type can annoy neighbours. Luckily for us, our nearest neighbour was over half a mile away across open farmland. Also, we were surrounded on three sides by woodland, which in my opinion should surely dampen any noise. Little did I know what the man from the Council was going to come up with.

Number 2 – Access. A Possible Danger?

Originally, our quarter-of-a-mile drive was a bumpy, potholed stoned track that accessed the main A41 highway. This particular stretch of highway was dead straight, where traffic could easily break the speed limit of 60 mph and illegally pass through the 100 mph barrier. This stretch of road was famous for young boys from my hometown Newport trying and usually achieving that wondrous feat of hitting 100 mph. (I am not going to admit if I was one of those boys!) I thought the access to the highway could be a concern with traffic entering or leaving our drive entrance. With bated breath, we could only wait as the Council considered our planning application.

In nervous trepidation, Kathy and I waited six long weeks to find out the result of the Council's decision. They seemed to be the longest six weeks in our lives. It is a good job I have never been into nail-biting because if I had I am sure that I would have bitten my nails right up to my armpits, let alone down to the quick. During those nervy six weeks, we had to post a notice of intention at the end of our drive, also in the local newspaper. This was to give anyone the opportunity to object to our plans. And sure enough, there was an objection. You always get one awkward sod. Don't you?

Well, surprise, surprise. The objection came from our nearest pet boarding proprietor who Dave the woodman had used for his German Shepherds. The protester claimed that there were already too many pet boarding establishments in the surrounding area. So why was it necessary to build a new one?

Well, he would do, wouldn't he?

We were astonished!

Of course, we knew his real reason for objecting. It was the fear of us taking some of his business away. Or maybe all of it! I don't suppose you could blame him. I am sure I would have done the same, especially when he could see that an ultra-modern posh establishment was going to be built only three miles up the road.

So, that was our first hurdle to get over.

The next step was a meeting with our architect and a Council member to prove that another boarding establishment was needed. To my surprise, the Council person turned out to be someone from my past. She was an old classmate of mine from junior school. Her name was Catherine. I knew she liked me at school or maybe even fancied me. Hey, I've always been a vain boy. So, I thought I would have a nice friendly chat with her. We spoke of our days at school, and I don't mean kissing behind the bicycle shed. Give me a break, I was only eleven! The conversation was about our classmates, what they were doing and where they lived. But Catherine soon clicked on and was having none of my creeping.

'Be careful here Geoff lad. This lady could turn out to be a real dragon!'

To be fair, Catherine proved to do a thoroughly professional job. To strengthen our case, I challenged her to check as many pet boarding facilities as possible in the area. My opinion was most of them were stark, cold and still in the dark ages. In reality, they should never have had a license. After recalling the 'Geoff Bond 008' reconnaissance, I convinced Catherine that a modern establishment was very much needed. I suggested in the future, maybe she would like to bring her dog to stay with us. And that is precisely what she did! Her dog's name was Henry and over the years he boarded with us frequently.

After my insistence that pet boarding facilities in our area were in the dark ages, Catherine said she would recommend that the objection be overruled. On hearing the mind-blowing news, I could have dropped through the floor!

Another Council member visited us concerning the noise level. His title was, Building Inspector. He arrived at Keepers Cottage with a roll of our plans tucked under his arm. He had no objection to the cattery building, which would be well away from the kennels, but he was very concerned with the noise level that the dogs could produce.

I was gob-smacked!

I said,

“But we live in the middle of nowhere and have dense woodland surrounding us on three sides. This site should be perfect!”

Showing no emotion, he pointed to the east at the panoramic view of rolling farmland and said,

“Yes, but noise can travel on the wind for miles over uninterrupted countryside like that."

To my amazement, he suggested that I should use expensive sound-damping materials in the building of the kennels.

‘What a shame it isn’t you paying for the bills mate.’

My fears were rising that this new venture would cost us an ‘Arm and a leg’ and take forever to build. Have you ever noticed how Council officials never mind how much of your money they can spend?

The architect had used my design, and from his drawings, the Building Inspector could quite clearly see that all the kennels were separated by four-foot-high walls topped with steel mesh rising to the corrugated fibreglass roof. If dogs wanted to see their neighbour on the right or left, they would have to stand on their hind legs, making it impossible for the smaller varieties, and for sure, the larger breeds would not be able to keep that strenuous position up for long. Also, regarding hygiene, the dogs could not pee into the neighbouring run because of the separating wall, instead of the steel mesh that most of our competitors had. Slowly but surely, the Building Inspector relaxed his official stance as he came around to my point of view. My mind was racing to try and think of a new idea that would please my newfound friend.

His frustrating suggestions were frightening me to death. So, I hit him hard. Not with my fists...

But with a brilliant idea!

Using my salesman's smile, I said,

"If the dogs can't see each other in the runs on the opposite side of the concrete aisle, maybe they will not bark?"

I suggested that I would rig up a giant sliding curtain that would hang down the centre aisle. My idea was, that if the dogs opposite each other could not see what was going on, it would stop them getting excited, especially during the dog walking sessions. The curtain would be made from a plastic tarpaulin that could be hosed down and disinfected whenever necessary. Also, it would act as a sound baffle.

With that, the Building Inspector thought all my ideas were more than acceptable.

Perfect, he wasn't a bad old stick after all.

So, it was 'Game On'.

In total, it was eight long weeks before we heard from the Council.

Finally, we got the planning permission!

Yes! Yes! Yes!

It was a tremendous relief to receive approval. The pet boarding license was granted for twenty-two dog kennels (block-built) with combined runs, plus thirty cat runs or, should I say posh compartments in a separate building (again block-built) more than 100 yards away.

It made my dream become a reality.

So, Geoff lad, you are now in business.

CHAPTER 3

Blisters on my Hands

I have always liked building and have completed house extensions, renovations, garages and sheds. You name it, I've done it. I have never had any problems with the labouring side of the building trade. I thoroughly enjoyed it. For skilled labour, I always hired subcontractors and for anything else that I could turn my hand to I did the work.

Stage 1

Initially, I needed to clear and level the ground. To do this, I needed a powerful machine, such as a JCB excavator. So, I looked in the good old Yellow Pages and found the nearest contractor, Lineal Construction. It happened to be in Newport, which was only just down the road. I made an appointment with the company director George, who happened to be a good friend of my father's.

George turned up at the agreed time to check out the ground and decide which type of machine was required. He decided a four-wheel-drive JCB would be more than adequate. So, there and then, I booked it for the following week.

My thoughts were excited with the prospect and momentum of building, but my main concern was the weather. The last thing we needed when the machine was working, was rain. I knew that if the ground got wet the heavy machine could quickly turn the large area into a quagmire. With bated breath, I watched every weather forecast for the coming week and prayed that it would stay dry. Let's face it, the United Kingdom is not exactly one of the driest places in the world!

During the week my job was to mark out where the kennel, staff room, toilet, office, and cattery buildings were going to be situated, plus the car park. I measured and marked out all the areas from the architect's plans with lines of white powdered lime.

As the week passed by agonizingly slowly, I continuously watched the sky and clouds with trepidation.

Finally, at 7:30 a.m. on a Monday, I heard the JCB's roaring exhaust getting louder as it came up our drive. My heart was thumping with excitement. The driver jumped down from his cab, and to my surprise, I recognised him. His name was Frank. Coincidentally we had attended the same school in Newport. After working as a lonesome gamekeeper for several years, I hadn't been in my new career for five minutes and I had already met two old-school pals. Catherine, from the Council and now Frank.

Frank quickly explained how he would tackle the job and then climbed back into his cab.

So, let the excitement begin!

The powerful machine roared and ripped into action bringing back fond memories of the Yellow Monster in the previous book. My Goodness, did I say fond memories?

Arghhh!

I have always found it quite fascinating to watch those powerful machines and the skills that the drivers have. As I watched the machine in action I was like an envious little boy. I couldn't take my eyes off it and after three hours the roaring JCB had moved the topsoil away quicker than fifty men could have with spades and shovels in three days.

Having finished the work where the kennel buildings, office, staffroom, toilets and car park were to be erected, the JCB moved down to the area where the cattery building would be situated. In just one day, the awesome machine had levelled the ground and prepared the foundations for both buildings.

Exciting stuff!

Here comes the second day…

I had made a no-charge agreement with a local farmer, Selwyn Jackson. The agreement was for him to bring his tractor and trailer to take away the rich topsoil. So, during the second day, the valuable topsoil was loaded by the JCB's powerful bucket and taken away to a nearby field.

Again, exciting stuff!

Wow! Now we have two attractive building sites.

Stage 2

This is where yours truly comes in for the concreting, which is backbreaking physical work. Having said that, I always found it immensely satisfying. To me, the look of recently laid concrete is beautiful, especially when you have just completed a long smooth stretch that glistens in the sunshine.

I started work on the cattery first, which consisted of two strips of concrete three yards apart. The identical concrete strips measured three yards in width and thirty yards in length. My first task was to provide wooden shuttering. I needed to peg down the shuttering to contain the runny concrete, actually a bit like a dam wall. The shuttering had to be level, with a slight fall running towards the centre. I have often found that the preparation always takes longer than the actual job intended. It took me three whole days, and I can tell you my days were long.

I purchased a second-hand electric cement mixer because I had decided to mix the concrete myself instead of using ready-mix. Little did I realise that I was making a big, big mistake. The local builder's merchants, Wheat and Kirkby, delivered the necessary sand, gravel and cement. With me being impetuous, I couldn't wait to get started.

The following day was bright and sunny. At 7 a.m. with my adrenalin flowing, I had the cement mixer going with the arduous task of shovelling the cement, sand and gravel in the correct measures into its gaping mouth. I was excited and enthusiastic as I wheelbarrowed the heavy concrete to the proposed runs and levelled it. I was shirtless and sweating profusely as 'I worked like a dog'.

Is that a pun, considering the business I was starting?

On that memorable day, Kathy had taken time off from work and had arranged for her family to come over for lunch. My Goodness, there was a tribe of them, consisting of Kathy's grandmother, who was almost ninety, her mother Isabelle and Kathy's two sisters, Audrey and Carole. They were all interested to see what we were up to or should I say, what I was up to.

I fooled myself into thinking I was making good progress, but a few hours later, when I stood back and observed what little I had achieved, I began to regret and realised I should have used ready-mix concrete. It had turned into a sweltering day with the sun beating down from a cloudless blue sky on my aching back. With the back of my hand, I wiped the streaming sweat off my brow and all I could hear coming from our garden were the envious sounds of laughter, accompanied by wine glasses clinking. Kathy and her family were having a good time and I wished I was with them. If only I had ordered ready-mix concrete I would have finished the job ages ago and be in the garden too. At least the girls did come over and offer me a glass of bubbles which I sensibly declined.

In dogged (another pun!) determination, I

struggled through the afternoon and by the evening I was wrecked, shattered, exhausted, you name it, that was me. And I had only completed three-quarters of the first run. I decided there and then…

I have had enough of this!

It didn't take many seconds to decide the rest of the concrete would be ready-mix. So, I made the call for a lorry load to be delivered the following day.

At eight-thirty the following morning, a large concrete lorry arrived containing six cubic meters of the lovely wet grey stuff. And within two hours I had levelled the lot. There is nothing like learning the hard way.

And boy, I just had!

Stage 3

The blockwork for the cattery.

This work was going to be a lot more straightforward, especially for me, because I would be the dumb labourer for my two 'brickie' friends, Eric and his mate John. (Brickie is the name given to bricklayers in the building trade.) Eric and John are the two guys that Sally my Springer Spaniel stole and ate their lunch in the previous book.

A large articulated lorry incorporating a crane turned up with an enormous load of building blocks stacked on pallets. It only took the driver twenty minutes to unload the heavy building blocks. But it took me eight hours of sweaty, backbreaking work to move them to the appropriate place from where they would be laid by Eric and John. There was no crane to help poor old Geoff, just my trusty wheelbarrow. So, I wheeled and stacked them in the exact spots where Eric had instructed me to do so for their block-laying convenience. Shortly after, another large lorry arrived with a big pile of sand and twenty bags of cement. All I needed on the following day were the two 'brickies', in the form of Eric and John, and then we would be ready to rock and roll.

The following morning, Eric and John arrived at 7:30 a.m. in a grey Ford van. They parked up, and with the van's radio blaring, they ate their breakfasts of delicious-smelling bacon sandwiches. I had already eaten my breakfast which was healthy cereal, but the smell of that bacon immediately re-awakened my appetite. But I hadn't got time for more food because the boys were to start work spot on eight. As they were eating and munching on those delicious-smelling bacon sandwiches and with me and Sally salivating, Eric gave me precise instructions on how to mix sand, cement and water.

Diligently following Eric's instructions, I poured a full bucket of water into the cement mixer and added a squirt of Fairy Liquid detergent. Amazingly, the detergent makes the finished mixture silky smooth. Who in the building world came up with that clever idea? To the water, I added one shovel full of cement and four full shovels of sand, then added a little more water. The consistency had to be just right, or they were not happy 'chappies,' and boy, did they make sure I knew about it! It wasn't because of any unpleasant threats, like sticking me upside down in the cement mixer. It was more like the rolling of the eyes, the whispers and the sniggering that rapidly turned me into an expert mixer of compo. (Builders slang for the mixture of sand and cement mixed with water.)

Boy, could those lads lay blocks fast? I could only just keep up with them.

After five hard days of sweat and toil the blocks were erected to make up the cattery walls. After another two days, the new walls were rendered on all sides with a mixture of sand and cement. Again, mixed by me. So, finally, after all our toil and sweat, standing on the two concrete strips was the skeleton of the cattery.

Wow, exciting or what?

Stage 4

Laying floor tiles, by yours truly.

This was just one of my many ideas to make the cattery look very smart, especially compared to other catteries in the Yellow Pages. Laying floor tiles was yet another job I had never attempted before. After explicit advice from Eric, I soon became quite proficient. What Eric didn't know about the building trade wasn't worth knowing.

The tiling was backbreaking and, even worse, knee-breaking because I spent virtually all my time kneeling. Thank Goodness I had taken Eric's advice and purchased some strap-on knee pads. After three long weeks, even after wearing knee pads, my knees were red raw and I felt I had a humped back similar to 'Quasimodo', the hunchback from Notre Dame.

Kathy and I chose a cream-coloured tile that would most certainly show up any dirt and also make each run very easy to keep clean, and even more importantly, germ-free. But wow, those tiles did make it look exceptionally spacious and I have to say very posh too. They looked fantastic. We were confident that our cattery would be the best in the country.

And as far as I am concerned, it was!

Eventually, it dawned on me that all the building materials were costing us 'An arm and a leg'. Every day, Kathy was driving a hundred-mile round trip to work in a large department of Barclays Bank in Cheshire. She was in charge of three hundred people and earning very good money. I felt guilty because I wasn't earning any money at all.

I was spending it!

I decided to revisit my double-glazing salesman's past and contact one of my friends, my ex-area manager, Ivor. He informed me that he was now selling central heating systems. And the good news was, the company was looking for more salespeople. The wages were excellent, and the work was in the evenings and weekends. These hours suited me down to the ground and because I had been very successful at selling before, the company took me on with open arms. Although I hated selling, we needed the money. So, I laboured on our premises during the day and went out selling for the heating company in the evenings, sometimes coming back as late as 2 a.m. The following day I started work at 8 a.m. Talk about burning the candle at both ends. I was absolutely shattered! I kept this up for a year, successfully selling the central heating systems and the much-needed money helped us tremendously.

Now back to my daytime job.

Stage 5

My next job in the cattery building was to erect the galvanised steel framework, the mesh doors and the see-through fibreglass sneeze barriers between each run. All these materials had been made exactly to my specifications. The entire framework was a daunting giant jigsaw puzzle.

Within five days of fixing screws, nuts and bolts, I had erected and fitted thirty cat runs, fifteen on each side. In front of the runs was a tiled path that ran around a three-yard space in the middle consisting of soil for an enclosed dwarf shrubbery. The idea of the dwarf shrubbery was to give the inside of our cattery a uniqueness that none of our competitors had. So now I had the cattery's shape to admire and my excitement was mounting more and more with each day and I just couldn't wait for the next day to dawn.

Stage 6

For the cattery roof, I used green translucent corrugated fibreglass sheets, which let the light and warmth in. The sun shining through gave the cattery a green warm glow. I read somewhere that green is the most soothing colour for a cat's eyes. So that's precisely what they got. And that was definitely going to be one of my future sales pitches.

To make the cattery totally secure (meaning no

escaping cats), I fixed a steel mesh frame to span the area between the lines of runs that faced each other. Below would be a dwarf shrubbery, so the mesh roof would allow rain to fall through naturally watering the plants below. Roofing was a job I had done before as I had built many sheds in my game-keeping days to house pheasants and partridges on the rearing field. I sailed through the fitting of the fibreglass sheets and steel mesh in only two weeks.

Stage 7

This stage in the proceedings was one of the more straightforward tasks that I had to contend with. Painting the walls white. I completed that job in a couple of days. Not bad going for an ex-gamekeeper. Mind you, in my time I had brushed creosote on hundreds of wood and mesh sections for pheasant pens, so I wasn't exactly a stranger to a paintbrush and I had always liked the smell of creosote.

Stage 8

I needed to assemble thirty cat boxes. These would be the sleeping quarters for each of our purring guests. The boxes were made to my design and were made of melamine, the same material used for various types of kitchen cupboards. I ordered cream-coloured melamine to match the floor tiles and had it professionally cut to my specified requirements. The melamine pieces stacked in three piles consisted of four sides, a top and a bottom. The bottom was much bigger than the top, forming a shelf for cats to sit at the entrance of their sleeping quarters. I tackled the three daunting piles of melamine, assembled them into cat boxes and fixed them to the back wall of each run that were elevated thirty inches off the tiled floor. Cats do enjoy being elevated and raising the boxes to that level ensured that our feline guests did not catch any draughts.

Stage 9

My next task was to make thirty small ladders, six inches wide by an inch thick. I made these from wooden planks and sawed them into the correct lengths. I then fixed one-inch-wide rungs, six inches apart to the planks. The ladders were for the cats to climb enabling them to easily enter their fancy sleeping quarters with an electric heat pad. I painted the ladders white to show any dirt and make them easier to clean and disinfect. It turned out to be a painstaking annual job because most of the cats used the ladders as scratching posts even though there was a scratching post inside each run.

A story about a cat that had a problem with my ladders is in a later chapter when the pet hotel was up and running.

Stage 10

Time to enlighten you about the shrubbery.

I planted numerous dwarf shrubs down the centre between the two rows of cat runs to soften the interior view of stark steel. Good idea. Don't you think?

Well, if you read the previous book in this series, you will know just how wrong one can be.

I purchased some beautiful shrubs from the local garden centre, supposedly the dwarf variety. The word dwarf is a clue to how wrong one can be. I painstakingly planted them down the centre aisle of the cattery building and between the shrubs I planted some mixed heathers. I covered the soil between them with beige-coloured Cotswold gravel which matched the beautiful cream tiles. It gave the cattery a lovely tranquil appearance.

Alas, another big, big mistake!

Initially, the shrubbery with Cotswold gravel looked beautiful, but it turned out to be a complete waste of time and money, which the next couple of years were so sadly to prove. But in the meantime, yes, we had a fantastic cattery, and the bonus was...

No one else had one like it!

The finished work in the cattery with colourful hanging baskets

Stage 11

Now it is the turn of our canine guest's accommodation. I started the mammoth task of building twenty-two kennels, an office, a kitchen, and a toilet. Don't worry, I will not bore you with another long-building episode, the process was pretty much the same as the cattery. The only difference was the time of year. By then we were well into the British wintertime.

In the kennel block, the roof was the biggest problem being four times as large as the cattery area and ten times fiddlier. It took me half of January and the whole of February to complete and it happened to be one of the coldest winters ever recorded. It was below zero every day with snowflakes spiralling and fluttering in the air. Boy, was it cold on those roofs and there wasn't a 'Brass Monkey' in sight, only poor me freezing my 'nuts' off.

At long last, by the end of March, all my building work was virtually finished. The biggest job left was to paint the kennels and the other buildings that were incorporated. I desperately wanted to catch the Easter trade and I had run out of time to complete the work myself.

I needed a professional.

So, I hired a painting contractor. Again, I was getting more excited by the day as we were getting very close to opening our very own pet hotel for cats and dogs.

And finally, after all that boring building stuff...

This is where the fun starts...

An eerie animal story follows...

CHAPTER 4

A Frightening Eerie Sound

MICK

It was a beautiful spring morning in late March. The birds were singing, the sun was shining in the clear blue sky and there was not one fluffy cloud in sight. It was the sort of day that made you feel light on your feet, almost as if you could fly with the birds leading me to think that I was going to have a brilliant day.

Today's plan was to hang baskets of flowers in the cattery building by using my new electric screwdriver. I was just about to leave the cottage and make my way to the cattery building when the phone rang in the study. As I talked to the person on the other end of the line, a short sharp sound erupted from somewhere outside.

"SCREEEEECH!!!"

As I talked on the phone, I wondered what the strange sound was, so I stretched over and opened the study window. I looked up towards the brand-new kennel block buildings, but the only thing that I saw was a blue car on the car park belonging to my painting contractor Dave. I had hired Dave to paint the office, staff room, toilet and kennels inside and out. On this day he was painting the inside of the kennel block.

Dave came and went as he pleased and it didn't matter to me what hours he kept. He had given me a price and promised it would be ready for the big opening day. Nothing unusual appeared to be going on up there, so I closed the window and finished my conversation. As I replaced the receiver and even with the window closed I heard the strange sound again, this time a lot louder and it sounded really eerie.

"SCREEEEECH!!!"

'That sounds horrible. What on earth is that?'

I ran outside to find out if an animal was suffering from terrible pain, but the only animal to be seen was Sally my faithful Springer Spaniel. She was trembling with her tail between her legs. I could see that she wasn't hurt, but whatever that sound was, it had undoubtedly terrified her. Also, I knew that she wasn't capable of making such a sound.

I stood still and listened...

The only sound was heavy rock music blaring away from Dave the painter's radio as he worked in the new kennel block.

It was very strange...

The birds had stopped singing!

Were they frightened as well?

A cold shiver ran down my spine.

'Geoff, pull yourself together and enjoy this lovely spring day.'

As I walked towards the cattery building with Sally, she was walking much closer than usual. In fact, she was brushing so close to my legs it was difficult for me to walk. As we entered the cattery, I heard a blackbird chirping away emitting his beautiful song.

I bent down and gently stroked Sally's head and said,

"Don't worry old girl. There's nothing to be frightened of. Listen, the birds are singing again."

Sally and I walked into the cattery building. I picked up my electric screwdriver that I had left on the top of one of the sleeping boxes. I attempted to erect the first wooden joist to support the hanging flower baskets that would bring some colour to the cattery. As I squeezed the trigger of the screwdriver there was a sound that would stay with me for the rest of my life...

"SCREEEEECH!!!"

The hairs on the back of my neck stood up. Sally ran to my side and tried to force herself between my knees.

‘*What was that?*’

Along with Sally, I bolted out through the cattery door. As we ran, I had great difficulty picking up any speed because I almost tripped over her with every stride. The poor old girl was only trying to seek more protection by being so close. But, the only sound that I could hear was more heavy rock music blaring from the kennel block. Also, I noticed the birds were quiet again.

What was going on?

And what on earth had made that awful screeching sound?

I hadn’t a clue from which direction the blood-curdling sound had come, and I didn’t know which way to look. And I can tell you, I wasn’t too sure if I wanted to find out. When I was a gamekeeper, I had heard some frightening sounds, but never anything quite like the one made that day. Strange sounds were quite normal in the countryside caused by various creatures. To a ‘Townie', the sound of stags in the rutting season might sound like a machine gun. A heron's harsh call might sound like a dinosaur.

Owls give a ghostly screeching sound. But in my opinion, a vixen (female fox) shrieking from close range was probably the most terrifying sound of all. None of those sounds frightened me one little bit. But nothing came close for me to figure out what this new sound was.

At least the daylight gave me the advantage of seeing what it might be rather than searching around in the pitch dark.

'But where do I look?

I wandered around, finding nothing, getting nowhere and getting no closer to finding out what it was or where the sound had materialised from. There was no more noise, nothing, absolutely nothing except the sound of Dave's radio blaring in the distance. I was baffled and frustrated and wasting my valuable time.

'Perhaps it has gone…Whatever it is, if it can make a sound like that, I don't fancy meeting it, even if it is in broad daylight!'

I went up to the kennel block to ask Dave if he had heard anything. He said he hadn't. Of course, he wouldn't have with his radio turned on at full volume. I couldn't even hear myself think! Tina Turner was blasting away singing 'Simply the Best'. I suppose Dave needed the volume turned up because he was deaf as a post. Anyway, I thought that if he had heard the eerie sound he would have come to me at the cattery to try and find out what it was. With mounting irritation, I marched back to the cattery to rescue what remained of my morning.

I gave Sally a stroke and picked up the electric screwdriver. As I squeezed the trigger, yes, you guessed it, what fantastic timing.

“SCREEEEECH!!!”

‘Someone out there is trying to take the pee out of me, that’s for sure.’

“SCREEEEECH!!!”

‘Maybe it’s Dave.’

Sally trembled with fear, but I wasn't the least bit frightened. Instead, I was getting mad. I decided that the only way I could find out what was going on was to stand outside and wait until the creature from hell or whatever it was let rip again. So, if it made the sound again, I would pinpoint which direction it had come from. I was at the stage where I didn’t care how much of my valuable time was lost. I was going to solve the puzzle if it killed me.

Did I say killed?

I crept around the area within a two-hundred-yard radius of Keepers Cottage for almost an hour. An hour I really couldn't spare. I heard nothing, saw nothing, and gained nothing. Except feeling a lot more peed-off than an hour earlier.

'It must have gone. Thank goodness for that. Now for Goodness sake Geoff, get back to work and forget it.'

"SCREEEEECH!!!"

'Surely, Dave must have heard that last shriek. It must have been heard miles away. Somebody is playing a practical joke here. It has to be Dave.'

I marched back to the kennels with Sally clinging as close to my legs as possible. I opened the door to the kennel block. As I entered, Dave was only just inside standing halfway up a step ladder and I could see by the look on his face that I had made him jump.

"Wow Geoff! You really gave me a fright."

I pointed at Sally, and with an annoyed tone in my voice, I said,

"You're not the only one who is scared around here."

He gave me a blank stare. I could see that he hadn't a clue what I was talking about as I tried to make myself heard over his blaring radio.

I shouted at the top of my voice,

“DAVE. HAVE YOU HEARD ANY STRANGE NOISES THIS MORNING?”

“NO, NOTHING UNUSUAL MATE. WHY?”

“OH, NOTHING MATE. FORGET I ASKED.”

I didn’t want to stop him from working, so I didn’t dwell on it.

I turned to walk away, and as I did so, I shouted,

“I’LL SEE YOU LATER DAVE.”

“YEAH. OK MATE.”

Dave went back to his painting and I left the kennel block more frustrated than ever. What a wasted morning. I decided to walk back to the cottage and have an early lunch. I was just going through the garden gate when…

“SCREEEEECH!!!”

I nearly jumped out of my skin, and Sally nearly jumped into my arms.

I spun around, half expecting to see some kind of monster stalking me. But there was nothing. As I looked towards the kennel block, I could see Dave walking away from his car, and as he saw me he gave a cheeky wave and walked back into the kennels carrying his lunch box.

'Right, that's it. It must be Dave. I'm going to get him back if it's the last thing I do.'

It was apparent to me that he had somehow been making that eerie sound all the time, and had been taking the 'Mick' out of me all morning. I had no idea how he had been able to make that eerie scream, but for sure, I was going to find out how, and pronto.

Dave had undoubtedly had a great laugh at me. I couldn't really blame him because I am a practical joker myself.

I suppose,

What is good for the goose is good for the gander.

As I ate my lunch my mind worked overtime thinking about how could I possibly pay Dave back, even if it was the only thing I would achieve that day. As I rushed my lunch down, I had a brilliant idea...

I unlocked my gun cabinet and picked up my double-barrelled twelve-bore shotgun. I grabbed two live cartridges from a carton of twenty-five and dropped them into my jacket pocket.

Carrying the shotgun in the crook of my right arm, I made my way back to the kennel block where Dave was probably eating his lunch. Within yards of the new office, I stood outside the entrance door to the kennels. I retrieved the two cartridges from my pocket and slid them into the chambers of the gun. I closed the barrels with a click and pressed the butt of the walnut stock tightly into my right shoulder in readiness to absorb the expected recoil. I raised the barrels harmlessly in the air and aimed over the top of the kennel block. Using my right thumb, I slid the safety catch forward cocking the powerful gun. With no hesitation I pulled both triggers.

BANG!!!!!!!!

BANG!!!!!!!!

The explosive sound echoed around the kennel block and surrounding woodland. Carrying the gun in my right hand, I rushed into the office and hid behind the door.

I didn't have to wait many seconds...

Dave hurtled out of the kennel block almost as if his backside was on fire.

Dave ran up to his car and walked around it with a puzzled look on his face. From my hiding place behind the office door, I watched him as he scratched the top of his head, obviously in deep thought. By sucking the top of my wrist, I was doing my utmost best to stifle my laughter. I could tell that he was wondering what had caused the twin explosions and where they had come from. I hid the shotgun which reeked of cordite behind the office door and acting nonchalantly, I strolled out of the office.

To make myself heard above Dave's blaring radio I shouted,

"WHAT'S UP DAVE? YOU LOOK LIKE YOU'VE SEEN A GHOST?"

Within a split second of the words leaving my mouth, a dreadful ear-piercing shriek exploded right behind me.

"SCREEEEECH!!!"

'Jesus Christ!'

I nearly jumped out of my skin. If I had a 'dickey ticker', I am sure I would have dropped dead on the spot.

Gathering my nerves together, I shouted,

"DAVE. WHAT ON EARTH HAVE YOU GOT IN THE KENNELS?"

"OH, THAT. THAT'S ONLY JANE."

"WHO IS JANE?"

"SHE'S MY DOG."

"IT SOUNDS MORE LIKE A WEREWOLF THAN A DOG."

"COME IN AND HAVE A LOOK AT HER MATE."

I followed him into the kennel block almost as if he owned the place, not me!

Halfway down the right-hand side in one of the runs was Jane. She was on her hind legs gazing lovingly towards Dave and was massive!

And the music played on...

I shouted,

"DAVE. CAN YOU TURN THE MUSIC OFF A MINUTE MATE? I CAN HARDLY HEAR MYSELF THINK."

"YEAH, OKAY MATE."

Dave turned the music off.

At long last, peace and tranquillity were restored. I no longer needed to shout and said,

"What sort of dog is that, Dave?"

"It's a Wolfhound?"

"Well, that's one of the biggest dogs that I have ever seen in my life. And I've seen a fair few in my time, I can tell you."

"You should see her catch rabbits mate."

"Wow Dave! She must be as fast as a cheetah. Rabbits won't stand a cat in hell's chance against her!"

"You're dead right mate. They don't. Me missus and me kids will never starve while me Jane's around."

"Have you got any neighbours near your house?"

"Na, nobody lives within alf a mile."

"I'm not surprised because if they did, they wouldn't stick around for long if Jane makes that awful noise. Anyway, why has she been making that blood-curdling shriek?"

"Oh, every time I walk out of the kennels to fetch summut or disappear out of sight, she misses me and just wails her head off."

I responded,

"I suppose you don't notice how loud Jane yowls because you're a little deaf. Aren't you, Dave?"

“What’d ya say, mate?”

‘I suppose that answer confirmed it.’

Everything from the morning's traumas fitted into place. I had solved the jigsaw puzzle at long last. The incredible sound only erupted when Dave was out of sight of his fearsome-looking hound Jane. And I have to admit that she was ‘As soft as a brush’, except with rabbits. I am ‘As sure as eggs are eggs,’ I wouldn’t like to be a rabbit when Jane was around.

Dave gave a mortifying statement,

“You’ll have to get used to this sort of noise when all these kennels are full mate.”

I looked at him gob-smacked.

‘Oh no! Surely not. What on earth am I creating?

My ambition was to have over a hundred dogs on the premises. Surely, they would not make a noise like Jane? Was I creating a monster or a business? Perhaps the building inspector was right regarding all of the rules and regulations about noise levels. All those negative thoughts flashed through my mind. I tried to dismiss them as quickly as possible because I needed to be optimistic about my new business.

'Please, surely there is only one dog on this planet that can make a noise like that and she is standing right here in front of me.'

Jane's long tail was swishing with her mouth gaping open reminding me of a crocodile. I am sure that she would have been able to hold two rabbits in her mouth at the same time!

Curious I said,

"Dave, do you ever go on holiday?"

"Na mate. I never have the time. If I get any time, I go off just for a day with Jane and the kids. It gives me Missus a break and keeps her happy. Anyway, it costs way too much to take me tribe away."

'At least I won't have to tell Dave any white lies. Meaning we were always going to be full where his lovely Jane was concerned. That was one dog for sure I would never want in my kennels. I knew there was no way I would have been able to stand all that shrieking. The thought was too dreadful for me to comprehend.'

Dave looked at me quizzingly and said,

"Oh, Geoff. Did you hear two loud bangs just before? It sounded to me like gunshots, but I think it was too loud for that."

"I never heard a thing, mate. Well, not above that terrible row your Jane was making."

With a puzzled look on his face, Dave stood with his hands on his hips. I winked at him, turned away with Sally by my side and headed back towards the cattery. I planned to sneak the shotgun out of the office later. At least Sally had met the awesome-looking hound called Jane, although she probably never realised that Jane had been the cause of the fearful shrieking sound. Just like me, Sally would have to get used to it and we would have to hope that Dave wouldn't leave the kennels too often.

To my surprise, the difference in size between Sally and Jane didn't stop them from becoming the best of pals, even if Sally did look like a toy dog in comparison.

In the evening when Kathy arrived home, I informed her about my eventful day and how the awful sound had really frightened Sally.

I joked,

"I think I'm going to buy Jane off Dave."

Kathy looked at me as if I had lost my marbles.

I continued,

"That hound is a million dollars on legs. I'm going to record Jane's voice and sell it nationwide as an alarm system to deter burglars."

Kathy laughed,

"You could be onto a winner there Geoff."

Because of Dave's words, the howling of Jane and my trepidation about the noise volume coming from a kennel full of Janes, I decided to install music in the kennels. I purchased a transistor radio for the grand opening and hung it halfway along the kennel block on a six-inch nail. There's nothing like being practical, is there? I thought, that if the dogs in the kennels could not hear what was going on outside, such as cars and people coming and going, they would not be disturbed and start barking.

Brilliant idea Geoff! I should have suggested it to the building inspector!

Virtually everybody has music playing in their home, so why shouldn't it make our canine guests feel less stressed when they are with us? And why not cats as well? So, I purchased another radio for them too, and as we expanded there was a radio for each new kennel block. It appeared the cats loved the music, the dogs loved the music, the staff loved the music, the customers loved the music, and being a pop fan, Geoff thought it was fantastic.

I often lay in bed with humorous thoughts picturing the cats and dogs boogying the night away.

Have you ever heard of radios wearing out?

Over the years, we wore them out.

Because we never turned them off!

Irish Wolfhound Facts

Originally, the breed was smooth-coated or rough-coated, only the rough-coated variety exists today. It is thought that Phoenician sailors brought dogs of greyhound type from the Middle East to Ireland and these dogs were crossed with Mastiffs to produce a dog of gigantic size with the speed and strength to see off wolves which were a great threat to livestock in Ireland. By the end of the 18th century, the wolf was extinct in Ireland and the Irish Wolfhound numbers dwindled. With the Great Famine in Ireland in the1840's the breed became very rare.

However, a group of devotees led by the Scotsman Captain George Augustus Graham, developed a breeding programme to revive the breed, with the few Irish Wolfhounds that had survived using outcrosses with the heavier type of Deerhound, the Great Dane and the Tibetan Mastiff. The Irish Wolfhound is reputed to be the tallest of the hound breeds and the biggest of all breeds. Despite their size, they are gentle, calm and truly a gentle giant.

The minimum height for male dogs is 31 ins (79 cm) and for female dogs, 28 ins. (71 cm) The Minimum weight for male dogs is 120 lbs (54.5 kg) and for female dogs, 90 lbs (40.9 kg)

CHAPTER 5

Crafty Maneuvers

MICK

We needed to create pet owners' interest in our exciting new business, and there were various ways of doing it.

The first significant thing I did was design a large sign to advertise our pet hotel. But, before I was able to erect it, would you believe? I even had to get planning permission for it. I had to fill in an application form for the Council which was much more challenging and complicated than you could ever imagine.

The sign had to be a specific size, the exact distance from the main road, a precise height from the ground, and the letters a specific size. The requirements appeared to be endless, but of course, I did what was necessary. The sign was made and delivered by Adrian my signwriter friend from the hilarious story in the previous book. I erected the sign on the grass verge (belonging to the Council) at the end of our drive, where it joined the A41 highway.

Finally, after all of that hassle, the sign with the exact specifications stood proud for everyone to see.

Then disaster struck...

Four weeks later on a dark night, the local students went on a drunken rampage and nicked all the signs along the A41 including our brand-new beauty.

'ARGHHH!'

I wasn't the slightest bit amused that my sign would be a trophy in some student's bedroom.

And for sure, I wasn't having it!

Just to jog your memory, I have repeated the following paragraph from the previous book.

There was a definite cure for this. So, what did good old Geoff do? He came up with the brilliant idea of fastening the replica sign with large nuts and bolts plastered with superglue and fixing it onto heavy steel scaffolding poles, that he had concreted deep into the ground.

Even today, when I drive past the end of our old drive, I see the sign standing there in all its glory. I wonder in amusement just how many night-time raids the students were frustrated with their attempts to take away sign number two!

Yellow Pages were one of the best instruments

we used for creating interest. I was delighted with the advert I designed. I knew it was completely different from the dozens of others portrayed by our competitors. All the other adverts were very much the same, describing what I thought amounted to a furry guest's stay in a stark-looking high-security prison.

Here is part of our advert...

SUPERIOR MODERN ACCOMMODATION IN A BEAUTIFUL TRANQUIL COUNTRY SETTING. WE ARE CONFIDENT THAT OUR PURPOSE-BUILT CATTERY & KENNELS WITH PANORAMIC VIEWS IN A GORGEOUS BACKDROP OF FLOWERS, LAWNS AND WOODLAND ARE ONE OF THE FINEST IN THE BRITISH ISLES.

I described our ultra-modern pet hotel as a luxurious place for cats and dogs to come for a holiday.

Here is another paragraph I used in Yellow Pages.

OUR BUILDINGS STAND IN A BEAUTIFUL, TRANQUIL SETTING, WHERE THE CATS ARE LOVED AND PAMPERED. THE DOGS ARE WALKED ON ARRIVAL AND THEN TWICE DAILY THROUGHOUT THEIR STAY. THEY ARE WALKED IN THE BEAUTIFUL SURROUNDING WOODLAND IN THE SHADE OF OAKS, ASH AND BIRCH.

Our establishment was a paradise for our furry guests. We even had a logo with a dog and a cat sitting in deck chairs holding cocktails. Well, we did provide the odd deckchair for both cats and dogs, but not the cocktails or champagne!

Our Logo

Numerous pet owners made this statement over the years,

"We'll stay here and send the cat and dog where we are meant to be going."

Over the following years, we advertised in Yellow Pages in four separate counties: Shropshire, Staffordshire, Cheshire, and the West Midlands. We took a half-page advert in each which was larger than any of our competitors and it stood out superbly. Throughout all the years in the business, we never changed that advert. To Yellow Pages, we were one of their biggest customers. In other words, we spent a lot of money with them. They treated us like VIPs and were always looked after by one of their senior managers. Unfortunately, Yellow Pages provided us with a different senior manager every year and it was Sod's law that the new manager always turned up at the most hectic manic time of the year...

August!

Well, they would do, wouldn't they?

I could never get them to come in November when I had plenty of free time. As the saying goes, 'When it rains, it pours'. Each year the new manager would suggest we change our advert. But no, I stuck to my guns. I knew it was an excellent advert and could not see how it could be bettered. So, 'If it ain't broke, why fix it'?

One of the questions a female manager asked,

"How many telephone enquiries do you get a week?"

I answered,

"Well, in the busy season, about thirty or forty a day and the majority of them book their cat or dog in."

Astounded, she almost fell off her chair and said,

"Good grief, that's unbelievable. I expected you to say two or three a week!"

Yellow Pages turned out to be an excellent tool for advertising. We gained more business through them than any other source. I am proud to add that ninety-five per cent of all inquiries wherever they came from were converted into new customers by Geoff, the ex-double glazing/heating salesman. I can assure you, that selling boarding facilities for cats and dogs was a walk in the park compared to selling twin sheets of glass in window frames or complicated heating systems. Also, what a fantastic environment I was in.

My third way of creating interest was to design a flysheet/drop card that could be posted through the letterboxes of the houses in Newport where I envisaged our early trade would come from.

I had 10,000 copies printed and coerced Ann, Kathy's sister, and Gail my sister, to help me and Kathy distribute them to the houses in the area.

Each night we went out to different areas and posted them through the letter boxes. It gave me great satisfaction when I asked a new customer how they had found out about us when they informed me that it was from the advertising sheet.

Also, after each new telephone booking, we posted the colour sheets as a brochure to that new customer.

Here is the sheet...

The fourth way of generating business was through recommendations…

And we got hundreds!

So, if you provide an excellent service, whatever business you are in, the recommendations will flow...

Another ploy I used at the end of each year was to ring our competitors and pretend to be a new customer. 'Geoff Bond 008' was spying again. It was a double-sided enquiry. Firstly, I was able to determine their prices for the coming year enabling me to adjust our prices accordingly. Secondly, it was to see how our competitors treated their new telephone enquiries. To my surprise, far too often, it took them two or three minutes to answer the phone, and occasionally it was never answered at all. Their attitude was off-hand almost like they were doing a favour by even talking to you. They sounded miserable or even downright arrogant. This is another reason why we were so popular. We were always very pleasant and helpful, no matter what task we might have been involved in at the time of the enquiry. Do you remember Sukie, the painful clinging cat?

My rule of thumb for staff was, please try and answer the phone within four rings.

With a mischievous look on my face, as a joke, I would say to a new member of staff,

"If you don't answer the phone within four rings,

you'll get the sack!"

I think they knew I was only joking.

The very first phone call I received for our new business was from Yellow Pages. I will never forget that telephone conversation. It came from Stafford fifteen miles away.

RING…RING…

Note that I only let it ring twice!

With mounting excitement, I picked up the phone and plunged straight into a full sales spiel. I explained to the person that she was speaking to the owner of probably the most prestigious pet boarding premises in the United Kingdom, if not the world. Now that got her going, I can tell you. I could be exaggerating just a little here!

I could hear the enthusiasm in her voice as she asked,

"Have you got a space left for my dog in August?"

Instantly, I realised that she had been ringing around, especially when she said 'space left'. Because of the school holidays, I knew that August would be the busiest month of the year. So, I have to admit, I told her a little white lie. I opened the blank pages in our brand-new unused diary for dogs, and as I flicked them over, making sure she could hear them rustling, I sucked in a deep intake of breath and replied,

"Phew, we are pretty full. What are the exact dates you require?

I could hear the mounting alarm in her voice.

She responded,

"I would like to leave my dog with you from the 7th of August and collect him on the 21st."

Again, making sure that she could hear, I fluttered the blank pages of the diary right down the phone's mouthpiece and again sucked in a deep breath as another little white lie left my lips,

"We've just had a cancellation for that period. It came in only fifteen minutes ago."

"I'll take it!"

Sounding cool, calm and professional, I asked,

"Can you please give me your name and address so that I can send you our booking form for you to complete and then when you receive it please return it with your deposit?"

She sounded quite panicky and with obvious

determination in her voice, she said,

“To make sure that I don’t lose that kennel space, I’ll send you my deposit by first-class registered post today and send you the completed booking form as soon as I have received it.”

She well and truly hooked.

After the conversation had finished, I placed the receiver in the cradle and punched my fist in the air and shouted,

“YES! YES! YES!”

I couldn’t wait for Kathy to come home to inform her loud and clear,

“We are in business. We have our very first customer well and truly booked in!”

CHAPTER 6

Our Very First Customer, the Scotsman and his Pugs

Pets come first.

Money comes second.

It was mid-April when the very first customer arrived on our car park. He was a Scottish gentleman named Mr Pageant. He had two toy dogs. They were Pugs.

Initially, I was working on my own, and the two little Pugs named Henry, who was a fawn colour and Timmy, who was a lot smaller and black.

The diminutive pair were very easy to look after and reminded me of Algy the Pug from 'Rupert the Bear Stories'. If my gamekeeper friends could have seen me walking those two toy dogs through the woods, they would have keeled over with laughter. It was undoubtedly a massive change from my normal macho Labrador and Springer Spaniel gundogs. Initially, Sally came on the walks, and I was sure she gave me some unusual looks.

The thing is, the macho ex-gamekeeper had to admit he actually enjoyed doing this special service, and secondly, getting paid for it. Henry and Timmy were two likeable little characters and they really grew on me during their two-week stay although I never went to the extreme of buying a pair.

The total bill for Henry and Timmy's stay came to a staggering sixty pounds. In those days it was an awful lot of money and I was dreading handing the bill to Mr Pageant. As most English people will have heard, the Scots have a reputation where parting with money is concerned. My golden rule was, you don't get your pets back until you have handed over your dosh.

I cringed as I presented him with the bill and stared in amazement because he never flinched. He merely glanced at it, wrote out a cheque and with no hesitation handed it over.

I looked at his cheque in awe.

'My Goodness, this is more than a week's wage when I was game-keeping.'

With my very first customer's cheque stowed safely away in my back pocket, I went into the kennels to put my mates Henry and Timmy on their leads and brought them out to their waiting owner. A beaming smile appeared on his face as he was taken aback by their contentedness and shiny coats. Also, he noticed how they were making as much fuss of me as they were of him.

After fussing and stroking the excited pair, he turned to me and said,

"Well Geoff, you have done a fantastic job. Here get yourself a drink."

To my amazement, he pressed a ten-pound note into the palm of my hand. After that momentous event, Henry and Timmy came to us for many years and Mr Pageant, their Scottish owner, always gave the staff a generous tip.

CHAPTER 7

Yes, of course, the Customer is Always Right!

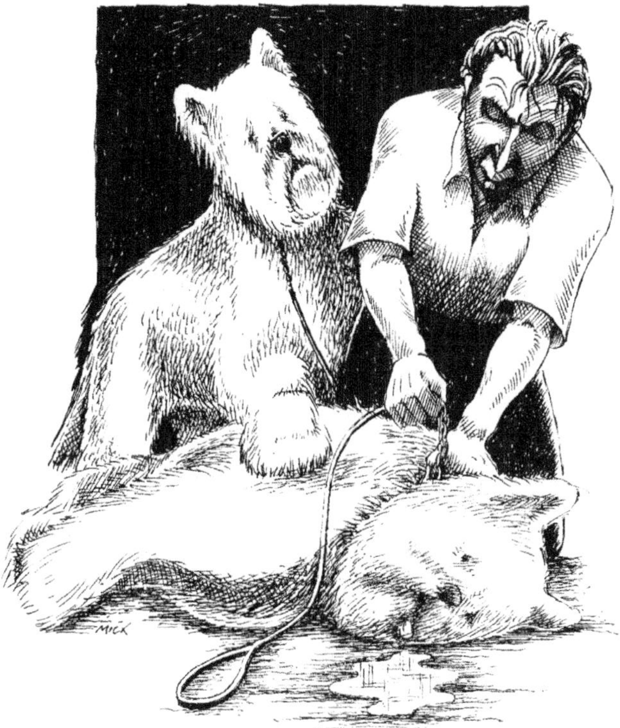

A very frightening experience...

There is a saying that my father used when he was a shopkeeper.

'THE CUSTOMER IS ALWAYS RIGHT!'

What he meant was, that customers could swear black is white and white is black, therefore you have to humour them. Even if you do not agree with them. With their money in your pocket, you just laugh all the way to the bank.

BUT THERE WAS ONE OCCASION WHEN SILLY, STUBBORN ME, IGNORED THE EXPLICIT INSTRUCTIONS OF ONE OF OUR VALUED CUSTOMERS.

Little did I know that my so-called superior knowledge was to land me in a very, very dire situation.

In fact, a double life-threatening experience!

A new customer rang me to book her two dogs in. It turned out that this lady showed her pair of dogs at Crufts and they had won many trophies.

The two unique-looking dogs were dark grey Briards.

In those days Briards were quite a rare breed in the United Kingdom. I had never clapped eyes on one, let alone a pair. So as far as I was concerned, they were as rare as 'hen's teeth'. As I spoke to this new customer and because I was running the 'best' boarding kennels in the land, I fobbed my way through our conversation. I am sure that when she put her phone down, she must have thought I was one of the most knowledgeable people on the planet where Briards are concerned.

So, what did I do next?

Yes, you got it.

I grabbed my trusty dog breed book to find out what the devil a Briard looks like.

Fact

Briards are an ancient breed of dog. They originate from France where they are quite common. They were originally bred for herding and guarding sheep. In the First World War, they were used for sentry duty and finding wounded soldiers which almost led to their extinction. In years gone by, Napoleon owned one and so did Thomas Jefferson the third president of the USA. A Briard's height varies between 23 and 27 ins (58 – 69 cm), they have a long course coat giving them a shaggy appearance which could be black, fawn, grey or blue.

After all that riveting information, here is my first Briard experience.

The very first time I clapped eyes on a Briard, I was on a skiing holiday in France. It was a sunny day and I was sitting at an outside restaurant having lunch with Kathy. On the other side of the road, Kathy spotted a strange-looking dog. At that time, I didn’t know what breed it was. To me, it looked quite comical with its shaggy brown coat and large floppy ears. It reminded me of a clown amongst dogs. Close by, were three other dogs. They were mongrel crosses. Unfortunately, they didn't seem to see the funny side of things and wanted to fight the clown-looking Briard, and sure enough a nasty fight started. Without thinking, armed with a ski stick and a very loud voice, I charged across the road to the fur-flying melee. Brandishing my ski stick in the air and screaming blue murder, I managed to break up the fighting four without getting bitten, resulting in the three cowardly mongrels high-tailing it down the road. The Briard appeared to look at me as if he was saying thank you. Then he wagged his tail inviting me to stroke his head. When I did, he wagged his tail even more and a crowd of on-lookers I hadn't even noticed, gave me a round of applause.

So, that is my first tale about a Briard with a happy ending.

The next one is frightening!

Knowing the owner of the Briards was a top show person, I knew she would probably be very fussy when it came down to leaving her two large hairy hounds with me. The day she arrived with the Briards she had a list of instructions in her hand as long as my arm. She read out every single word in a very formal posh voice. I thought she sounded just like the Queen.

Anyone would think that I couldn't read!

When she had finished, she handed me the list.

For sure I was going to obey her every command.

WELL, ALMOST ALL OF THEM!

Her parting command was,

"They do pull a bit, but don't use a choke chain on them, because it can tangle in their coats."

After that posh command, I decided to nickname her the 'Queen'!

If you haven't realised, I do like nicknames!

The 'Queen' eventually left, leaving me standing on the car park with her two 'Princes'.

As she drove away she appeared to be eyeing me suspiciously in her rearview mirror.

I had a horrible feeling from her expression that she was thinking,

'Does this guy know what he's doing?'

I sincerely hoped that wasn't the case.

OF COURSE, I KNEW WHAT I WAS DOING!

One of our girls Tracey, was walking from the cattery towards the kennels.

I called,

"Hey, Trace. Can you get me two choke chains, please?"

Choke chains do stop dogs from pulling and they also stop them from slipping their leads and bolting away from the stranger on the other end of the lead, meaning me or my staff. The last thing I needed was her two valuable hairy hounds disappearing over the horizon. I am sure the 'Queen' wouldn't have hesitated in ordering me to be beheaded if I had lost her pair of valuable 'Princes'.

So, I put the chain necklaces over the heads of the very excited Briards. They were obviously raring to go for a walk. Suddenly, the 'Princes' got really excited and started to dance merrily around on their hind legs as they wildly looked around probably wondering why 'Her Majesty' had left them with a strange peasant. I was quite determined that they were not going to escape from my clutches as I was about to take them for their introductory walk in the woods. (Do you remember Skip, the Houdini Hound in the first book of this series?)

Not over my dead body!

DID I SAY DEAD BODY?

I think it should have been more like dead bodies.

Take note.

Bodies is the operative word.

Because...

I couldn't believe my eyes!

Before I had even started to leave the car park, one of the hairy 'Princes' started to cough and choke like mad.

And when I say choke...

I MEAN CHOKE!!!

The idiot was doing his best to strangle himself on the other end of the lead as he pulled, writhed and twisted against it, which I, the greatest dog-walking expert in the world was holding.

'What a great advert this is. All I need now is a

customer to drive onto the car park and see me killing a dog by strangulation!'

I was doing my utmost not to panic.

I tried, but could not get my fingers under the choking chain, especially with 'Prince Two' pulling like mad on the other lead.

I shouted to Tracey who had no idea about my predicament as she was about to enter the kennel block,

"Trace! Get over here quick. I've got a big, big problem."

Tracy ran over with a look of horror on her face.

I said,

"Here, Trace grab this lead."

She grabbed hold of 'Prince Two's' lead who was twisting, pulling and panicking on the other end.

By this time, Prince One' was rapidly going weak at the knees.

And so was I!

HE WAS GOING DOWN!!!

The choke-chain was...

STRANGLING HIM!!!

OH, NO!

HE IS DYING!!!

Tracey was hanging on to struggling ‘Prince Two'.

Tracey shouted,

"LOOK GEOFF! This one has got the same problem. The choke chain is tightening and twisting in its hair."

I turned around and couldn't believe what I was witnessing...

‘Prince Two' was choking and going down as well!

I YELLED!!!

" PLEASE DON'T DO THIS TO ME!"

The 'Queen' had only been gone two minutes and it looked like she was going to be the only survivor of her Royal Family.

Oh no! Her valuable show dogs would be dead before she got a mile down the road.

'Prince One' was down on the deck with his eyes rolled back...

Only the whites were showing.

For sure, he was going to die!

And I felt like following him!

What was I going to do?

The more I tried to free the chain the tighter it was getting and the coarse hair was knotting up all around it.

I looked around to check 'Prince Two' and...

Jesus Christ, he was down on the deck in a mirror image.

'Oh no! Surely this can't be happening. Why on earth hadn't I listened to the Queen?

I promised myself there and then, if I got out of this one, I would always obey whatever the customer instructed.

Then an idea hit my brain like a thunderbolt.

My toolbox was only yards away in the kitchen and I had a pair of robust wire cutters in it.

But the question was...

Would they be strong enough to cut the two choke chains?

Well, there was only one way to find out...

Run and get them!

I left the two dogs lying and dying with a shell-shocked Tracey on the car park.

Like greased lightning I bolted for the kitchen and with the wire cutters in my hand I exploded back even faster.

I landed next to 'Prince One' in three bounds, the poor chap was lying on his side and looked as dead as a doornail.

Frantically, I attacked the offending silver chain with the wire cutters and inflicted as much strength as Tarzan.

I could feel the metal yielding as I squeezed…

Suddenly…

The silver chain snapped with a dull click.

'PRINCE ONE' REMAINED MOTIONLESS!!!

I had to leave him!

No time for the kiss of life…

I rushed over to 'Prince Two'.

Maybe, I could at least save one of them.

He was lying on his side.

There was life in his eyes!

HIS EYES WERE ROLLING!!!

With all my strength, I squeezed the cutters…

There was a resounding click…

The silver chain broke.

HE WAS FREE!!!

He was going to live!

For sure, I saved his life!

But I wasn't too sure about mine!

Tracy shouted,

"GEOFF LOOK!"

Reacting, I turned around.

To my amazement...

'Prince One' was standing shakily on all fours.

His tail was slowly wagging.

I could have kissed him!

If he hadn't got up, kissing him would have been my final plan. In desperation, I would have definitely tried to give him the kiss of life.

Can you imagine one of our customers driving

onto the car park and witnessing me giving a dog the kiss of life.

Well, at least I hoped that was what they thought I was doing...

The mind boggles!

Within a minute, 'Prince Two' was also up and running with his docked tail wagging.

Immensely relieved, I looked at the two 'Princes'.

I said,

"I think I've just saved your lives, lads."

They looked up at me and I was sure if they could have talked, they would have answered,

"Yes, and you nearly killed us, you idiot!"

After that frightening experience that should never have happened, the three of us went for a walk around the woodland circuit with them back on their OWN leather leads! It seemed that they had forgotten all about their more than exciting episode on the car park as they walked along wagging their stumpy docked tails just as if nothing had ever happened. The Briards were meant to be staying with us for three weeks, and I had nearly killed them in three minutes! That surely would have been some sort of record, not to be proud of!

Well, their story didn't quite finish there...

After our little ordeal, I had really gotten quite fond of them and it was ten days into their stay when Jenny, shouted,

“GEOFF QUICK. YOU NEED TO SEE THIS.”

Have you noticed that I do a lot of running or even sprinting in my stories?

I arrived in seconds.

Curious I asked,

"What's up, Jen?"

"It's your two hairy friends. They have diarrhoea!"

“WHAT! I don't believe it. Out of all the dogs in here at this moment. It would have to be these two."

I took one look at them and said to Jenny,

"I think they have gastroenteritis."

With no hesitation, we attached their leads to their collars and bundled them into the back of my Daihatsu 4 x 4 to drive them straight down to the veterinary surgery three miles down the road. Before I left, I made a brief phone call to confirm that there would be a vet available with it being out of normal visiting hours. With Jenny in the front passenger seat, I pulled up outside the surgery in record time. We rushed the two sick dogs inside where Mr Bishop, the vet was waiting.

He confirmed exactly what I thought and said,

"It is just a mild form of gastroenteritis, nothing too serious."

And thank goodness for that!

After a couple of jabs and some pills twice a day, they were as right as rain, and after a few days, they were eating and crapping normally again.

On the morning of their collection, the girls bathed, blow-dried and groomed the pair of Briards. Later that day, the 'Queen' came to collect her two handsome 'Princes'. They had been with us for just over three weeks and 'Queeny' was over the moon with them.

In her posh royal voice, she congratulated the girls and of course, myself and said,

"Oh, my boys look absolutely wonderful. They look like they are ready for Crufts! I can't thank you enough."

'I'm glad your boys can't talk. They could certainly tell you a tale or two!'

After our initial strangulating ordeal, the hairy pair boarded with us on numerous occasions.

And the three of us kept our dark secret.

To put the top hat on it or should I say, the crown.

The 'Queen' and I became good friends.

Mind you, I never had the courage to confess about the near strangulation of her pair of 'Princes'.

Or my nickname for her!

A beheading in the Tower of London comes to mind!

So yes Dad,

'THE CUSTOMER IS ALWAYS RIGHT!'

CHAPTER 8

Spots Before Your Eyes

This story is about a horde of horrible intruders invading our beautiful cattery.

For the essence of this story, I need to point out that the cattery has thirty walk-in runs with cream-coloured ceramic tiles.

When you start your own business from **scratch**, very often you have to learn things the hard way. There is nobody there to give you any advice, therefore we learned new things at the pet hotel almost every day. By the way, the word **scratch** is very appropriate to this story.

I DO HOPE YOU ARE NOT SQUEAMISH!!!

This story happened in the early days when I was still on a big learning curve. During the week, I worked alone. The weekends were busier and that is when Kathy helped along with a couple of local schoolgirls.

Occasionally, when I was working alone in the cattery, I found tiny spots on the cream floor tiles. The spots were reddish-brown and looked a little bit like fly dirt. But I thought no more about it. Subsequently, as the business grew we had a lot more cats to contend with.

AND THE REDDISH-BROWN SPOTS GOT MORE FREQUENT!!!

Also, we noticed that there were tiny brown specks that looked like large dust particles, or even fine particles of soil. The specks were no bigger than a pinhead. In some instances, they were all over the floor, especially if two cats were sharing the same run. Of course, two or even three cats sharing the same run were from the same household. For sure, we did not mix strange cats as some unreputable catteries in our area did. If we had, I hate to think what we would have found after a night of catfights.

Naively, we thought that all the dirt was from the cat's fur. I imagined that they had probably been rolling about in a flower bed before they came to us. Let's face it. Who knows what cats get up to during their night time forays?

On one particular day, I was asked by our schoolgirl helpers Jenny and Gill to come to the cattery and inspect the tiled floor in one of the runs. The run contained two cats that had arrived only the day before. Jenny and Gill were keen to show me the state of the floor tiles before they cleaned them.

I stared in horror at the cream tiles.

Well, they were cream yesterday, but the horrible sight that greeted my eyes today was absolutely disgusting.

The once beautiful cream floor tiles were covered in reddish-brown spots. The spots were much bigger than any I had seen before. Some of them were a similar size to the top of a pencil and appeared to be more like splashes.

The horrible part of this was…

Even to the untrained eye…

The red spots looked like…

Blood!

'Oh, No!'

IT WAS BLOOD!!!

'Oh no! These cats are bleeding to death!'

Gently, I picked up each cat and carefully examined them. Both cats seemed to be okay and I could not see any wounds or blood coming from either of them. They looked really healthy and had eaten all the dried biscuits from their morning meal. The cats were brother and sister and there appeared to be no antagonism between them. With them being totally unmarked I was certain that they had not been fighting. I thought, perhaps a mouse had wandered in from the bordering woodland and they had been lucky enough to have had some live food as a tasty extra titbit that wasn't on our menu. Anyway, there seemed to be nothing to worry about, so I gave the okay for the girls to go ahead with the cleaning.

The very next morning, Jenny and Gill were greeted with the same bloody (to coin a phrase), problem again. Lo and behold, the cream tiles were tarnished with the same bloody mess.

That was the only and best way of describing it.

A BLOODY MESS!

Something was taking the blood from these two cats and I wanted to know exactly what it was.

By now, I was thinking along the lines of...

Vampire bats!

I knew vampire bats did not inhabit our country. They come from South America. Perhaps some stupid idiot had been keeping vampire bats as pets and one may have escaped or even worse…

Released on purpose!

Well, your imagination can run amok.

Can't it?

An evil looking Vampire Bat

'Maybe one of our vets can throw some light on the subject?'

Without wasting a moment, I sprinted up to the office, grabbed the phone and rang the veterinary surgery.

One of the three partners, Mr Edwards answered.

Trying to catch my breath, I said,

"I think something is taking blood from two cats that came in a couple of days ago. There are blood spots all over our floor tiles."

In a nonchalant tone, he answered,

"Oh, that's a simple problem. They've only got fleas."

On hearing that statement I was mortified.

'Fleas! Fleas! They've only got fleas! How can fleas in my cattery be a simple problem? What is this simple problem going to do to our reputation? If this simple problem gets out to the public, we'll be dead in the water!'

All these thoughts were flashing through my mind. I tried to think calmly. I suppose it could be much worse, a flea problem was far better than a vampire bat problem!

But why did I have to get the problem just when the business was steadily building up?

I asked the vet,

"How do we eradicate these fleas?"

I sure hoped it would be a lot simpler solution than, vampire bats!

He answered,

"All you need is a special spray. It comes in an aerosol can and it is called Nuvan Top. You simply spray the infected cats all over. But be very careful not to get it in their eyes."

He never mentioned ours!

"Do you sell it?"

"Yes, of course. We have plenty in stock."

"I'm coming down, right now."

I banged down the receiver, raced to my vehicle and drove down to the vets like a madman. I was back in record time with three cans of flea-killing spray.

The vet advised me that I would need two people to perform the operation.

A simple task, he made it sound.

Perhaps he had not met as many little 'tigers' as I had!

So, this is what the vet advised...

With gloved hands, one person was to pick up the cat by the scruff of its neck and place the other hand under the base of the tail to take the weight. As the cat was suspended the person with the spray would shield the cat's eyes with one hand and then aim and fire the can with the other.

It sounded quite simple, but time would tell, and for sure, I did not like the idea of picking up a struggling cat by the scruff of the neck one little bit.

As I was about to perform this potentially dangerous operation, I was hoping that my blood wasn't going to join the cat-biting flea splats.

IS ANYONE ITCHING YET?

BECAUSE I AM!

This was the start of my first exciting exercise

of spraying a cat and hopefully eradicating the nasty parasites. So, I armed Gill with the aerosol can and made it abundantly clear,

"It is the cat that has got the fleas. Not me!"

I reiterated,

"Just make sure you watch where you are pointing that thing!"

I had no idea how the first cat was going to react when I picked it up by the scruff of its neck and more importantly what its reaction would be when we started spraying it.

I imagined a full-scale war would erupt.

Well, here goes.

'No guts, no glory'.

Gently, I slid my hand around the back of the cat's head and stroked our furry guest or should I say the first guinea pig. I wanted to let him know that I was friendly and wasn't going to hurt him. Enjoying my stroking, he started purring. With him being so relaxed, I located the loose skin on the scruff of his neck and gently grabbed it...

Then swiftly and smoothly with my other hand supporting his rump, I picked him up.

It was unbelievable.

No reaction!

No reaction at all!

To my surprise, the cat went completely placid and tucked his back legs up just as if I was going to carry him off to somewhere safe. Probably like his mother did when he was a kitten.

Ok, so far, so good.

Now it is time to introduce the aerosol can...

Gill had the aerosol can hidden behind her back because we did not want to frighten the poor little chap before we even got the process started. It could have possibly made him go a tiny bit berserk!

And believe me, you do not mess with berserk cats!

Gill introduced the can.

Guess what?

No reaction!

No reaction at all!

To our amazement, when we sprayed the flea-ridden cat he never even batted an eyelid. He remained perfectly calm and allowed us to spray him all over.

I smiled at Gill and our spectator Jenny who was keenly watching the proceedings.

With a smile on my face, I said,

“Well, that was a piece of cake. Okay, next cat please.”

Knowing animals like I do. I could have virtually guaranteed that the next cat would not be so placid.

As per usual, thank Goodness, Geoff was wrong.

We were amazed, the second cat did a repeat performance as its companion.

Then it hit me…

Not the cat, the idea.

These cats have been sprayed before!

It was blatantly obvious that these cats had been sprayed by their owners on a regular basis probably from when they were kittens.

Hey, I am itching as I write this!

Anyway, no major cat war had occurred and as a bonus, none of my blood had been splattered all over the cream tiles.

And more importantly, I hadn't been sprayed either!

The first thing the following morning, I couldn't wait to get to the cattery and check the tiled floor of the run belonging to the sprayed cats. I entered the cattery and quickly walked along the path to check their run. To my relief, it was spotless, not a disgusting blood splat in sight.

So, it became routine. If the cream tiles were splattered with blood the morning after a cat had arrived, it was zapped immediately with the magic spray. Cats only needed just the one zapping and they were free from the horrible parasites. But, that only lasted until the cats went back home where they would be able to roam wherever. No doubt they would hunt and catch mice, shrews and rabbits that are infested with fleas and the disgusting cycle would start all over again.

After our very first case of fleas, we decided that we would never tell any of the owners that we had sprayed their cats. I am sure it was the right decision. We knew it was impossible for cats to get fleas in our cattery. I had built it with no nooks and crannies where fleas could hide or lay eggs. As soon as any cat was collected, the area was totally disinfected.

TAKE NOTE ALL YOU CAT LOVERS!

At least fifty per cent of the cats that came to board in our cattery were infested with fleas. Because of our vigilance and our cream tiles, there was no way any cat would ever leave our premises with the horrible bloodsucking parasites living in the dense fur.

A magnified flea, probably full of blood sucked from its host.

Have you had an itch or a scratch as you are reading this? I have!

The sad fact is, cats obtain their little passengers from the small mammals they kill!

Wild rabbits fur crawls with fleas and even moles that live their lives virtually one hundred per cent underground can carry the horrible biting parasites. So the fleas riding on their host (your cat) into a warm house where there are fitted carpets... Arrive in flea paradise. Deep pile carpets are an ideal place for fleas to lay thousands of eggs.

'ARGHHH!!!'

And pest-control companies spray houses for fleas, week in and week out.

For me, the most alarming thing about fleas is that they often carry tapeworm larvae in their blood. When the flea bites a cat, dog, or any other animal, that horrible larva transfers itself into the animal's bloodstream and that is why you have to worm cats and dogs regularly. Even worse, we can be bitten by the horrible blood-sucking parasites and humans have been known to have tapeworms over twelve feet long basking and feeding in their intestines! Whether humans obtain tapeworms from fleas, I don't know, but it doesn't even bear thinking about.

I started to itch when I was writing this story and I am sure itching now!!!

Unfortunately, especially for me, not all of the cats had been sprayed before they came to board with us, so it wasn't always so easy to handle and pick them up. If it looked like we were going to become worse off from the occasional spitting, hissing bundle of fighting fury we sprayed those cats without handling them. We did this by cornering them and giving them a squirt with the magic spray. Often, they wouldn't stand still, especially when somebody was spraying a strange-smelling liquid at them.

Well, would you?

I got quite adept at hitting a moving target, (almost like a clay pigeon) spraying an airborne cat as it flashed past me in its run was some sort of experience I can tell you. I was always very careful to avoid the cat's eyes and of course my own. I knew the spray stung because I had been hit several times by the girls.

I have to say, the girls were not as good a shot as me!

It wasn't so easy to tell if a dog had fleas, but I can assure you if a cat came in with fleas and the owners had a dog boarding with us, we zapped that as well. Our reasoning was, that if the cat had fleas, then the dog living in the same household would most certainly have them too. I can verify that because if I go back to the very first cats that I sprayed and there was a dog from the same family boarding with us, I checked it out by examining the ears (a favourite place for fleas to congregate) and yes, the dog was covered in the nasty parasites.

And oh my Goodness, the bedding had tiny specks of blood on it too!

My very first experience of spraying a dog with the magic zapper was yet another exercise when I wasn't too sure how the dog would react.

Would it bite me, or the girl that was helping me?

Would it go berserk?

One of my girls Haley volunteered for the task at hand. We discussed how we were going to go about it. After our discussion we decided, I would hold the dog by the collar because I was the strongest and Haley would do the zapping.

I made this joke every time,

"Now just remember Haley, it is the dog that has the fleas, not me!"

Well to our utmost pleasure, it was a piece of cake. This dog had obviously been sprayed before.

After all our zapping the good news was we never had one complaint about a cat or dog leaving our premises with fleas.

I know to this day that if a cat or dog had gone home with the nasty blood-sucking parasites infested in its coat, their owners would have blamed us for it.

So be warned, if your cat or dog is scratching a lot, especially the ears, it could well have fleas.

Are you itching now?

Well, you should be!

I will now explain how fleas manufacture and produce spots of blood, whether they landed on our cream tiles in the cattery or on the carpets in your clean house.

The fleas carried by your cat or dog are non-stop sucking and feeding on your pet's blood. Now and again the cat or dog will shake or scratch its body quite furiously. It is quite normal for cats and dogs to do this whether they have fleas, or not. Just like a person having a good old scratch. So when a flea-infested cat or dog shakes or scratches, some of the flea poo which is the end product of the host's blood is eventually shaken off.

So, in the cattery, we were lucky because the flea crap in the form of red spots was splattered onto our cream tiles which were easy to see.

Now your carpet is 'A different kettle of fish' because more likely than not, you won't be able to see any blood or even worse...

Flea eggs!

So here is a warning to all you cat and dog owners.

If your pet goes outside and has anything to do with small mammals, especially rabbits, then you must spray them regularly because those blood splats could be going all over your lovely carpets or even worse...

Your bed!

Don't take my word as gospel, speak with your vet and I am sure he or she will tell you the same thing.

It doesn't bear thinking about. Does it?

Surely you are scratching now!

And, what about the good old tapeworms residing in human intestines?

Now that is food for thought!

CHAPTER 9

Four Shaggy Irish Leprechauns

This is a horror story!

You may well ask, what does an Irish Leprechaun have to do with dogs?

Well, the four dogs in question in this story were Irish and smallish.

Now, with those two words Irish and smallish you will notice at the end of each word, the three letters ISH.

This new word ISH is a word that Kathy and I picked up when we were on holiday in Southern Ireland for the first time.

For example, the Irish people might say,

"I will be with you in five minutes...ish"

Or, on the outside of a pub door, there would be a sign...

PUB NOTICE

OPENING HOURS

OPEN TWELVE…ISH
CLOSED TEN…ISH

Now that is what I call an enviable laid-back way of living.

For me, that is one very good reason for liking the Irish, I just love the word 'ISH'.

And of course, there is the Guinness!

Yes, I know, there is no ISH on the end of Guinness.

The very first pint of Guinness I savoured was in Temple Bar Dublin with two lovely Irish friends David and Dawn. We met them years ago when they were on their honeymoon in Greece and we have remained close friends ever since. It is down to David that Guinness is my favourite drink. Also, he introduced me to the Irish drink of Potcheen (alcohol content 40 to 90 per cent), but that is another story. Or should I say, a drunken story!!!

Interesting facts about the history of Poitín/ Potcheen

Poitín (Irish pronunciation) Potcheen, is a traditional Irish distilled beverage (40 to 90%)

alcohol content. Former common names for Poitín were 'Irish Moonshine' and 'Mountain Dew'. Traditionally it was distilled in a small pot still and the term is a diminutive of the Irish word 'pota' meaning pot. The Irish word for hangover is 'póit'. In accordance with the Irish Poitín/Potcheen technical file, it can only be made from cereals, grain, whey, sugar beet, molasses and potatoes.

Anyway, after that fantastic piece of information about the Irish language, Guinness and Poitín/ Potcheen, I will now get to the heading of this dramatic short story.

Four Shaggy Irish Leprechauns

Well, the dogs in question may not have been Irish Leprechauns, but they were certainly Irish, small... ish, ginger... ish and shaggy... ish, in fact, they were four Irish Terriers.

Not many people have ever heard of the breed Irish Terrier and have no idea what one looks like.

And I have to admit, I was one of those people.

At that time, they were very rare indeed.

Fact

The Irish Terrier is a dog breed obviously from Ireland and is described by an old Irish writer as being the poor man's sentinel, the farmer's friend and the gentleman's favourite. They are considered to be one of the oldest Terrier breeds in the Canine Kingdom and are very active. A compactly sized dog that is suited for life in both rural and city environments. Its harsh red (ginger... ish) coat protects it from all kinds of weather. These dogs were bred, not just for their looks, but more for their working qualities and are ferocious rat killers like their brethren the Jack Russell.

An Irish Terrier generally has a golden or red shaggy coat and stands quite tall for a breed of Terrier. They are about 18 to 20 ins (46 to 51 cm) in height, compared with that little demon the Jack Russell which averages around 12 ins (30 cm). Hey, and if you think a Jack Russell has a temper, in comparison an Irish Terrier's temper is double. An Irish Terrier also goes under the name of daredevils by dog fanciers. Irish Terriers can be very aggressive to other dogs, but generally not to humans. People who don't know any different would probably think of the word Irish Terrier as an Irish man with a terribly aggressive or fighting nature. Well, the Irish

Terrier has certainly acquired that reputation and I might add from my experience in this story, that is a very fitting description.

This breed of Terrier fears absolutely nothing above ground, especially if it has four legs. They would take on a fight with any other dog, no matter how big the breed.

Irish people aren't like that at all.

Are they?

Well, certainly not with my experience with Irish people, and I have never met any real Leprechauns. More is the pity.

Many an Irish man or Irish lady has similar hair colouring to the breed of Irish Terrier. Perhaps that is where the similarity for a bad temper arises. It is often said that redheads have a fiery temper. From whatever country they come from.

Hey, I am more than happy that Kathy is blonde!

When the owner of four Irish Terriers, Mrs Kerry phoned me to make a two-week booking, I quickly flicked through the pages of my book of dog breeds. For sure I didn't want to let my new customer know about my naivety. (Remember the Briards.)

Mr and Mrs Kerry owned four of the rare breed, consisting of three dogs and a bitch. The Irish Terriers were show dogs and what is more, they had won many trophies between them and therefore they were quite valuable. I was soon to meet this breed in the flesh for the very first time. And I have to say, I will never forget them!

Mr and Mrs Kerry arrived on the car park at the agreed time in a gleaming silver Mercedes Estate. Pat and I greeted them and welcomed them into the office. As we checked the vaccination certificates and booking forms, I looked out the office window and noticed the four Terriers were in separate travelling cages in the back of the car.

With the paperwork out of the way, the couple went to their car and put the four Terriers on leads. For some reason, they wanted them walked separately and then handed them over to Pat, Tracy, Haley and me. As we chatted on the car park, the couple proudly informed us what great individual champions the Terriers were. As I admired the gang of four, I could just imagine them in the ring at Crufts standing proud and erect.

The couple informed us that they had chosen our

boarding kennels because we had been highly recommended by other show people who had been using our facilities regularly for a number of years. So of course, I proudly accepted their compliments with a big smile on my face.

Then I said,

"I noticed that the Terriers have travelled in four separate cages."

It was a question that I had already guessed the answer to.

Mrs Kerry answered,

"Yes. That's because if they start fighting, they just won't stop until one of them is severely injured or even dead."

She added,

"They could do untold damage to each other, possibly scarring each other for life."

'Ugh, ugh we had better be ultra-careful with this load of nutters.'

With those alarming thoughts in my mind, I said,

"I think it would be wise to put them in separate runs."

I wasn't surprised when the couple unanimously agreed with my logical advice.

So, that is exactly what we did. Also, I made doubly sure that all the staff were well aware of the importance of keeping these valuable dogs well away from each other. I decided the gang of four were going to get the VIP treatment that they deserved because I was going to be one of the four to walk them. And you can bet your bottom dollar separately! This was to make absolutely sure that their two-week stay with us was uneventful.

And it was!

On the gang of four's collection day, they were bathed and groomed ready for Mr and Mrs Kerry to pick them up. When they arrived and paid their bill, we led the gang of four out of the kennels and the couple commented that they were delighted with the condition that the Irish Terriers were in.

And as a bonus, they left a very nice tip for the girls.

Four months passed by before the gang of four were with us again. But for some unknown reason, Mr Kerry wanted the dog and one of the bitches boarded together in the same kennel.

Perhaps he was trying to keep the cost down.

Well, we did offer customers a considerable discount when dogs shared.

On the day that they arrived, I could tell that his wife wasn't too happy with the two Irish Terriers sharing the same kennel.

I strongly recommended that they should have separate kennels, clearly remembering what Mrs Kerry had told me on their first visit. But Mr Kerry was having none of it and was quite adamant that the two dogs should share.

So that is exactly what we did.

But...

I had a foreboding feeling...

I could sense a pending disaster!

'Don't forget Geoff, the customer is always right.'

After all, they were his dogs not mine, so he should know them inside out.

As long as they weren't going to tear each other...

INSIDE OUT!!!

Maybe, I shouldn't have had a thing to worry about, but I still had my doubts.

Perhaps I should have ignored his instructions and gone along with my gut feelings and separated them. But the problem in doing that was there was not a kennel free because we were so busy. Therefore, we could not take the risk of moving someone else's dog to share with a canine stranger as this could have created even more problems.

So, we ended up doing exactly as the owner Mr Kerry instructed.

Still, staying on the safe side, the Irish Terriers were walked individually, as we had done on their previous stay.

Well, we got through day one...

No problems at all.

Day two, three and four...

No problems at all.

A week passed...

No problems at all.

Another week passed...

No problems at all.

So great, no problems.

They were going home the next day.

I decided, that if they used us again because of my sleepless nights worrying about what grim scene I might find the next morning, I would make absolutely sure that there was an extra kennel free. Even if the owners still wanted them to share, I would keep them separate, it just wasn't worth the risk and worry.

'Forget charging them the extra money for the extra kennel.'

Early on their morning of departure, I entered the kennel block with more than my usual feeling of trepidation. I walked with tentative steps to the three kennels that the Irish Terriers were occupying...

I stopped dead in my tracks!

'JESUS CHRIST!'

I couldn't believe what I was looking at...

Have you ever been to an abattoir?

It is a place where they kill animals for meat.

Well, I haven't!

But I imagined what confronted me could have been an equal.

Probably an abattoir would have been more pleasant to look at.

I had never seen so much blood in my life.

I didn't think so much blood existed on the planet!

The scene in front of me looked like someone had lost control of a crimson paint sprayer.

Or...

Even, a blood sprayer!!!

There was not a place on the Irish Terrier's concrete floor where you could place your foot without standing in blood. The ghastly red stuff was splattered up the walls and there were even red splashes and streaks on the underside of the roof which was more than six feet high.

The dog and bitch were thankfully...

Still alive.

BUT ONLY JUST!!!

Motionless, they stood side by side.

They were panting heavily.

Their blooded tongues lolled out from the side of their pink frothed jaws.

Both Terriers were covered in blood from head to toe.

Both were totally exhausted.

Both had given as good as they had got!

And to put the top hat on it...

If they survived!

They would be finished for showing.

That's for sure!

'OH, NO! NO! NO! WHAT AM I GOING TO TELL THEIR OWNERS?'

The other two Terriers on either side in adjoining runs were equally exhausted.

THEIR FACES WERE COVERED IN BLOOD!

Obviously, the spectators had been standing on their hind legs in a bid to get over the separating wall to join in the epic battle next door. Their facial blood must have been splashed or squirted from the fighting dogs during their frenzied attack on each other.

'Oh, no! They are being collected in four hours!'

'What am I going to do?'

'Why hadn't I heard the racket that they must have made?'

'What on earth were the owners going to say?'

Before I called the vet, I decided to separate the panting fighters. As I went into their run they wagged their docked tails, albeit feebly and were 'As quiet as church mice'. My goodness, they did look a sorrowful sight. As I separated them, I felt very sad and disappointed. Gently, I ushered the male dog into the sleeping quarters, turned the light on and bolted the steel door behind him. Then I left the awful scene with the badly wounded female dog standing and shivering in her run.

I ran for the phone.

'YOU MAD IRISH IDIOT'S.'

To his credit, the vet dropped everything and was with us in twenty minutes. Myself and my horrified staff helped him clean the blood off their coats. The pair of Irish Terriers never flinched as he stitched up their wounds. They just stood there like the proud warriors they were.

The vet said,

"I think these wounds will heal well and once the stitches are removed the scars should soon disappear."

Relieved, I said,

"Does that mean they will still be able to compete at shows in the future?"

He answered,

"I don't see why not."

I could have kissed him!

Well, at least that was the first bit of good news I heard that day.

But, and it was a very big...

BUT!

I was certainly not looking forward to facing the music when the battle-torn warriors were picked up by their owners later.

Not one iota!

Also, it might be just a little bit embarrassing to hold my hand out and ask for the bill to be paid. But after all, it was not my fault because against my advice, Mr Kerry had strongly insisted that the crazy Irish pair should share the same kennel.

Inevitably, Mr and Mrs Kerry turned up three hours later in their Mercedes. I think they could tell that there was something very wrong when they looked at my face, which according to Pat in a conversation later, was 'As white as a sheet'.

I stammered, in embarrassment,

"I am so sorry. The dog and bitch have had a fight, either during last night or in the early hours of this morning!"

Without hesitation, Mrs Kerry turned towards her husband and snarled,

"I told you so. I knew they wouldn't last all that time together without fighting."

'These two are going to be fighting as well in a minute!'

Trying to calm things down, I said,

"Don't panic. The vet has been and said that they only have minor wounds. But if you could have seen the amount of blood, you would never have believed him. I had a terrible shock when I walked into their kennel block early this morning."

I felt quite mean by saying those words, but it was his fault they had been fighting not mine and it was 'Muggins' here who'd had all the trauma and worry.

I added,

"The good news is, the vet reckons that you will still be able to show them in the future."

On hearing my optimistic words they calmed down.

Now it was the husband's turn to have a white face!

Sheepishly he said,

"Can we see them?

'NO WAY.'

'Not before you pay your bill first mate!'

As my confidence started to grow, I asserted my authority and said,

"I think it would be best if we completed the paperwork first and then I will bring them out one at a time."

That meant, paying me quickly!

Like, right now!

As they were paying their bill, a very subdued Mr Kerry asked,

"What about the vet's bill?"

"Don't worry, I will see to that. I will claim it back on our insurance."

'Great! That'll put my insurance premium up!'

If only he had listened to his wife and myself, none of this would have happened.

But of course, the customer is always right...

BUT NOT THIS TIME!

After all the paperwork was sorted out, (meaning me getting paid), I fetched the Irish Terriers out one at a time. First and second to make an appearance were the two unharmed spectators from either side of the gladiatorial fight. As they were fastened in their cages in the back of the Merc they looked immaculate due to our conscientious staff who had bathed and groomed them.

Next, it was the turn of the two fighters.

Again, one at a time.

The wounded pair, except for a bit of limping, didn't look that much different from the pair that hadn't been fighting. The only difference was, the warriors were wearing Elizabethan bucket-shaped white plastic head collars to prevent them from licking their wounds and pulling their stitches out.

I overheard Mr Kerry whisper,

"They look better than the last time they fought."

I couldn’t believe what he had whispered. I was absolutely speechless.

Surely, it hadn't happened before.

My mouth dropped open, but no words came out. I wanted to give him the biggest telling-off in his life. Or should I say, the biggest rollicking of his life, but I just stared at him in amazement.

Anyway, I didn't need to worry. His wife did the telling-off for me. As they walked towards their car, she launched into a full-blown verbal attack.

'Serves you, right mate!'

If it hadn't been for another car drawing onto the car park, I'm not sure what she would have said or even done to him. As she jumped into the Merc she slammed the door so hard, I thought it was going to come off its hinges.

Or, even break the glass.

Silently, Mr Kerry got into the driving seat and I could see her glaring at him. If looks could kill, he would have been dead on the spot!

As the 'loving couple' (I don't think so) drove off, I could see her hands gesticulating.

I said to Pat,

"Well, we have had some Irish blood spilt today, it looks very much like there may be some English blood spilt as well."

Smiling at my joke, Pat and I turned away from the departing car to greet the new customer.

So, the Irish Terriers very much left their mark on us or should I say in their kennel.

Even if it was the mark of...

BLOOD!

I suppose it could have been much worse, all four could have been boarded together!

The good news to end this story is, that the vet was right, the 'loving couple' were able to enter the Irish fighters in the show ring again.

Phew!

What a relief that was!

After that Irish Terrier horror story, it is time for a bit of fun concocted by my staff and me in the next chapter.

CHAPTER 10

It's Only Love

A practical joke on Kathy!

This story is about a lovable dog called Sam. 'LOVABLE', is the operative word.

Sam was a powerful Dalmatian. He inherited his strength from his ancestors who in the late seventeenth century were bred for trotting alongside horse-driven carriages belonging to aristocrats.

Interesting facts about Dalmatians

Carriage drivers noticed that dogs and

Dalmatians in particular, had a very calming effect on their horses. The use of Dalmatians trotting with horse-driven carriages carried over to the horse-drawn wagons that firefighters rode to the scene of a fire. When a fire alarm sounded, the Dalmatians ran out of the firehouse barking to let bystanders know that they should get out of the way because the firefighter's horse-drawn wagon would soon come roaring by. Once the wagon was out on the street, the Dalmatians ran beside it. The brave loyal dogs served an important purpose once the wagon approached a fire. Horses are afraid of fire, and the Dalmatians' presence distracted and comforted them as they pulled the wagon closer to a blaze. The Dalmatians also stood guard near the wagon to ensure that no one stole the firefighters' belongings, equipment or horses. Nowadays, Dalmatians are mascots for the fire services in America.

Dalmatians have also been war sentinels, circus performers and hunters. No one knows for certain where the breed originated, but Dalmatians are named after Dalmatia, a coastal area that long ago was part of Austria. Dalmatians are thought to be descendants of the pointer. Amazingly, Dalmatian puppies are born white, without spots and the pattern of spots on adults is unique to each animal. At one time a Dalmatian held the record for giving birth to the largest litter of puppies, 19. That record was broken in 2004 by a Neapolitan Mastiff which had 24. The stamina and endurance of Dalmatians is amazing. Their height ranges from 19 to 23 ins (48 to 58 cm). Unfortunately, almost a third of Dalmatians are deaf or have hearing impairment.

After those amazing facts about Dalmatians, here is Sam's story...

The Dalmatians we know today are primarily companion animals. And, Sam certainly loved companions...Especially the female variety!!!

Sam was as handsome as any Dalmatian could be. I'm even sure he fancied himself the way he strutted around so arrogantly and he always seemed to have a knowing glint in his gorgeous big brown eyes. Knowing Sam as I did, he probably sat in front of the patio window at home admiring his reflection for hours on end.

I even thought about putting a mirror in his kennel!

Yes, he was a very proud lad indeed. This guy would be able to pull any bird on the planet. Sorry, I mean female dog. But this handsome white, black-spotted creature wasn't interested in any breed of dog...

He was kind of...

DIFFERENT!

Sam was very, very interested in birds alright, not the feathery type, more the human variety!

He was a real 'Casanova', or so he thought. But I must say where I was concerned, he was an absolute gentleman. Sam just happened to like girls more. But the trouble with him was, he could get just a little overzealous. In fact, on occasions, his gentlemanly conduct could disappear right out of the window.

For sure, the kennel maids had to watch him.

Because, this big strong, handsome lad had ambitions!

You could certainly say that again!

As you can imagine, none of the girls wanted to walk the lecherous Sam which was not all that surprising. As handsome as Sam was, you couldn't blame them. I mean girls don't go for boys with spots. Do they? Well, in his defence his black spots were beautiful, not like those of the weeping red-yellow-headed acne variety!

But Sam you are a dog mate. Girls do not fancy guys with four legs!

So, with Sam having no loving tendencies towards me, I walked him most of the time. But, if he had tendencies towards the male gender, then perhaps even I might have thought twice about getting too close to him.

We did not put any information about Sam's lechery on the blue card (blue for a boy) attached to the gate of his run, it was common knowledge to all what Sam was really like.

Well, it was common knowledge to all but one...

And that just happened to be my innocent Kathy!

Just to jog your memory, Kathy is five foot five inches tall, slim but not skinny, with long blond hair, rosy cheeks, hazel eyes and more often than not, sporting a big beaming 'Cheshire Cat' smile.

Kathy had been away all week working for Barclays in London and was helping us on a very busy Saturday afternoon. Unfortunately, Sam's taste in ladies was something that had slipped my mind. Well, don't blame me! I didn't keep the general knowledge about Sam's lecherous inclinations from the love of my life on purpose. I mean, would any guy keep secrets about a handsome Dalmatian from his wife? Certainly not me! I have always had my wife's best interests at heart.

Kathy, having just walked Sam's next-door neighbour, a yellow Labrador, spotted...

Did I just say spotted?

The drop-dead gorgeous Sam.

So, she decided to take the handsome beast for a walk in the woods.

How does that well-known nursery rhyme go?

Oh, yes! It has come to me.

'If you go down to the woods today, you are in for a big surprise'.

But it was me that was surprised.

Because...

Nothing happened!

The odd couple completed their walk and Sam

had behaved like a true Dalmatian gentleman. He hadn't even laid one aristocratic paw on my beloved Kathy. In my anticipation of some humorous action, along with two young staff, we watched furtively from the office window. We had a full view of the line of runs as we watched Kathy and her handsome spotted beast approaching down the centre aisle.

She led him into his run and slipped his choke chain over his head.

Ugh! Ugh!

The removal of the choke chain had a strange effect on Kathy's spotted friend.

Here we go...

An evil, lustful glint came into Sam's sparkling eyes as he manoeuvred himself between the gate of his run and the girl of his dreams. (Well my dreams actually.) Perhaps that sentence in brackets has hopefully got me out of a bit of trouble!

In his excitement, Sam was wagging his tail furiously. He only had eyes for Kathy.

He homed in on her like a guided missile.

Kathy, not quite realising what was going on in Sam's head or any other part of his body, patted him on his back which I am afraid he must have regarded as some sort of invitation.

Sam's passion was running high and he looked gleefully into her eyes with his large pink tongue lolling out of the side of his quivering mouth.

She turned her back on him to leave his run.

But...

Sam could not wait a moment longer...

He launched himself from behind...

He reared up onto his hind legs and wrapped his front legs around the top of Kathy's arms, pinning them tightly to her body.

Finally, it dawned on Kathy just what Sam's true intentions were.

Kathy could feel his hot breath on the side of her face and he was slobbering on her shoulder.

She shouted,

"GET DOWN SAM!"

I am sure Sam was thinking,

'*Hey Kathy, I know you're playing hard to get, but I love you and you're not getting away from me now!*'

Kathy could do nothing to stop him, his weight was pressing her against the mesh gate and for some reason she looked towards the office window.

We ducked down, but too late…

I could see that she had seen me laughing along with my two young accomplices and realising the joke she started to laugh.

She shouted,

"OKAY GEOFF, I GET THE JOKE. NOW COME AND HELP ME. I CAN'T MOVE. THIS SEX-CRAZED NUTTER IS CRUSHING ME TO DEATH."

We were in hysterics as we watched Sam and Kathy dirty-dancing heel to paw. Sorry, I mean in Kathy's case. A wrestling bout!

Still laughing, I said to my partners in crime,

"I suppose I'd better go and rescue her before I get into some serious trouble."

I walked into the kennel-block trying not to laugh and approached the two lovers who were locked in a waltz dancing faster than ever around Sam's run.

Amazingly, Kathy was laughing and shouted,

"WILL YOU PLEASE GET THIS SPOTTED MANIAC OFF ME?"

I am sure that there could easily have been some much stronger words in that sentence. So, without offering her a hand, I turned my back and started to walk away, again trying to hide my laughter.

Kathy couldn't believe I was leaving and shouted,

"WHERE ARE YOU GOING NOW?"

"I'm going to fetch my camera."

"GET BACK HERE. RIGHT NOW, OR I'LL KILL YOU!"

Now she was getting serious.

Well, I was only joking, I wasn't really going to fetch the camera, but it would have made a very interesting photo. Now Kathy usually has lots of patience and I knew by the tone in her voice that it would be better for my future survival to help her, the 'Damsel in distress'!

So, I about turned and like a Knight in shining armour, I charged to the 'Damsels' rescue.

But, rescuing her was not the easy task that I had envisaged.

I entered Sam's run and tried to grab his incredibly strong front legs which were clasped tightly around Kathy's upper body.

I couldn't believe it…

He growled at me!

GRRR!!!

For sure, he was not going to share her with anyone!

It didn't matter to him that this lovely lady was married to me; he was going to have her at all costs. It must have looked quite an amusing spectacle to see a married couple and a Dalmatian dog doing the foxtrot or should I say the Dalmatian trot in a kennel run.

Without getting bitten, I could not release Sam's tight grip from around Kathy's body.

GRRR!!!

I said,

"I'm sorry, but cold water is the only answer."

"You can't be serious!"

"Have you got any other bright ideas? Honestly, I can't get him to release you and I don't fancy getting bitten by this nutter in the process.

GRRR!!!

"Oh, do it then. Just get this idiot off me. At least I've got a waterproof jacket on."

GRRR!!!

Well, I'm sure everyone has heard of separating dogs with buckets of cold water!

GRRR!!!

Before I got myself in deep water with Kathy, I vacated Sam's run at speed to retrieve, not a bucket of water, but something that would be a lot more accurate. Initially, I thought of the power hose, but I decided to use the hosepipe. I thought it would be a little gentler on the two revolving lovers.

I turned the tap on full blast. So, with the long hosepipe in my hand and cold water splashing around my feet I ran back to Sam's run to rescue my Kathy.

GRRR!!!

I entered the run where the two lovers stood heel to paw, but the question was, how was I going to achieve a separation of bodies without getting Kathy wet? I had to cool down Sam's ardour somehow and it needed to be quick, so I pelted him on his private parts half splashing Kathy with the icy cold water.

It worked!

Instantly, Sam released his grip and dropped down on his front paws.

He gave me a very sheepish look as if to say,

"Spoilsport."

Or maybe it was,

“You swine!”

Sam slunk off to his sleeping quarters and was probably contemplating what might have been.

And I faced Kathy’s wrath,

"You swine, my jeans are soaked and I've even got water in my wellies.”

Trying to defuse my situation I laughed and said,

“At least I rescued you. You could have been having some spotted puppies if I had let him carry on.”

“You knew he was like that, didn’t you, you pig! Why didn’t you or someone else warn me?”

Feigning an innocent look on my face, I said,

“Well, he hasn’t done anything like that before. Certainly not with me anyway.”

I was doing my best not to laugh as I tried to get

myself out of deep water or I could have ended up wetter than Kathy!

Angrily, Kathy said,

“You’re obviously not his type! Are you?”

“Well, there is no doubt about it you certainly are.”

“I’ll get you for this Geoff, I really will. You just wait and see.”

Now, this last statement did worry me a little bit because Kathy always paid her debts. I tried not to think about future cold showers or anything else that might have been even worse. At least Sam justifiably deserved his cold water treatment.

I mean, whatever had I done wrong? Apart from forgetting to mention Sam’s amorous tendencies towards young ladies.

I wouldn’t do that on purpose.

Would I?

Well, just to round off Sam’s love story.

I informed his owner about the spotty lad's ambitions or should I say to clarify his amorous advances on my wife. He couldn't help but laugh the way I told the funny story.

When he finished laughing, he said,

"Actually, Mr Doody I'm glad you told me because Sam is sometimes a bit like that with my wife and we have seriously been thinking about having him castrated. I know he's not normally aggressive, but he seems to think it is some sort of game. Do you think it will stop him from being like that if we get the vet to give him the chop?"

I replied,

"Well, yes, it quite often does calm dogs down. If you don't intend to breed from him, then maybe it wouldn't do any harm to get him seen too."

On Sam's next visit, I felt sorry for him because the poor lad was minus two parts of his anatomy. His owner said it had calmed him down a lot and Sam had stopped letching his wife. Also, Sam appeared to have an even nicer temperament than before. All this good news was relayed to Kathy, but she never chanced walking him again.

She never forgot that big bear-hug, or should I say, Sam-hug he had given her.

I fet so guilty about Sam being so placid after having his bits chopped off.

All I can say is…

Sorry, Sam!

CHAPTER 11

Collecting and delivering, not one of my better ideas!

This is an amusing story about Geoff's great idea...

A collection and delivery service.

Is it a great idea?

Well, we shall soon see...

When we first started the business, I collected and returned customer's cats and dogs. I soon found out the real reason why customers liked my service. It took a great deal of my time instead of theirs. When I started my new business, I went to all sorts of lengths to encourage more trade. I am sure it wasn't that our customers did not have time to drive the love of their lives to and from our premises. I think it was because they preferred to let their cats and dogs, vomit, pee and poo inside my vehicle instead of their own.

On numerous occasions, I collected two tabbies named Topsy and Turvey and a Beagle named Bertie from the same household.

This story is about the very first time I collected the trio.

After my first journey with the trio as passengers in the back of my vehicle, why I ever did it again I will never know. But I must say, they were always as good as gold when they boarded with us.

The owners of Topsy, Turvy and Bertie appeared to be quite wealthy, especially with their house or should I say mansion along with the expensive vehicles parked outside. Two of the cars consisted of a Range Rover and a Mercedes Sport. Adorning both cars were personalised number plates and there were two other smart cars that probably belonged to their grown-up children.

I was due to pick up the trio late on a Friday afternoon. It had been a cold wet autumn morning and it was getting dark earlier than usual. The autumnal wind was blowing a hooley, with yet more cold hail coming down like stair rods. I left our premises driving my faithful Daihatsu 4 x 4, thinking at least it was the perfect vehicle for the job. I was quite naive in those early days concerning our collection and delivery service. And didn't know quite what to expect.

I arrived at the 'mansion' and was greeted enthusiastically by the owners. I scrutinised the trio's three vaccination certificates.

No problems there.

So, I opened the back door of my vehicle and loaded two heavy cane wicker baskets containing Topsy and Turvey. Then I ushered the very excited Beagle named Bertie into the back. And boy, the way he started jumping around, he appeared to have more energy than Skippy the bush kangaroo. (Skippy was a children's Australian TV series.)

Take note. Originally, Beagles were bred for hunting and have boundless energy. And in this story, Bertie is right up there regarding the energy factor.

I closed the back door and not taking any chances locked it, jumped into the driver's seat and with the first turn of the key fired up the engine engaged first gear and slowly drove away.

I was only five minutes into my journey with Bertie nonstop bouncing about.

When it hit me…

'*What on earth is that vile smell?*'

Quite simple really!

It was just plain good old-fashioned cat crap. It smelt so foul, that I'm sure I could almost see it in the air.

I could even taste it in the back of my throat!

I don't know what had caused the cat or cats to go to the toilet in my Daihatsu. Yes, my lovely Daihatsu that had recently been refurbished. For sure, I most certainly wasn't too happy about it.

Whether the cat-crapping incident was caused by the sound of heavy hail hitting the vehicle like a staccato of machine-gun bullets. Or, the crazy Beagle bouncing all over the place and jumping on the two cat baskets.

I just don't know.

But something I did know.

It stank to high heaven!

Bertie for sure, was certainly doing his utmost to capsize the wicker baskets in his excitement to get to his new destination.

That first vile smell was soon to be added to by a second vile smell...

Cat pee!

And we all know what that smells like.

Well, if you don't?

Just imagine mixing the two vile smells in a very confined space that you cannot get out of in a hurry. I can assure you that it made a bad smell in a lift quite a minor event in comparison!

In front of me, I had a twenty-minute journey of twisting country lanes with high hedges that were covered in lethal wet leaves.

Therefore, I had no escape from that excruciating pungent smell.

So, there was nothing I could do. I just had to put up with that awful smell that was wafting from behind me. Well, at least I was separated from the trio by a mesh dog guard.

Actually, awful does not even come close to describing how bad that smell was.

I could almost taste it!

The other thing I tried to achieve, was not to breathe in too deeply. In fact, I imagined I was swimming underwater and tried not to breathe at all.

I drove my 4 x 4 so fast that I thought I was in the wrong occupation. I could have won rallies with the skills I had that evening.

The stronger the smell...

THE FASTER I DROVE!!!

My main worry, as I drove the drive of my life that seemed to be going on forever, was...

Would Bertie the Beagle crap as well?

And if he did, what kind of new smell was I going to be greeted with?

As I sped along, all I could think about was the smelly scene that was undoubtedly going to be waiting for me when I finally arrived at my destination and opened the back door of the Daihatsu.

Then things got worse...

Now the nutty Beagle behind me was flying at the dog guard.

And...

Oh no!

Yapping as well!

Bertie, just never let up with his excitement as he bounced around throughout that memorable journey.

Anyway, the good news is...

I achieved that ordeal in fifteen minutes when it should have taken twenty!

Thank goodness, I didn't meet any other vehicles on those dark, wet, twisting leaf-covered roads.

Arriving in front of my office in a calculated skid, I evacuated my vehicle faster than a pilot ejecting from a crashing fighter plane.

Ignoring Bertie's excited yapping, I stood in front of the office trying to gather my senses as I breathed in deeply to savour the sweet country air. Procrastinating, I was dreading to contemplate what kind of disaster was waiting for me in the back of the Daihatsu.

I had forgotten what it was like to breathe normally. And wow, did that air smell and taste good.

Eventually, I gathered my senses and nerve then walked around the back of the Daihatsu to grab the rear door handle. As I inched the door carefully ajar, my little friend Skippy, sorry I mean Bertie attempted to thrust his little black shiny nose through the narrow gap.

But, I was more than ready for him!

Believe me, I for sure wasn't going to get myself

covered in cat crap, dog crap or pee from his flailing paws. At that moment, the bonus was, I hadn't sensed the smell of dog crap amongst the concoction of smells that my more than sensitive nose had picked up.

There were times like this when I wished I had a smaller nose!

Bertie was getting better by the second at impersonating a kangaroo, so I quickly lassoed my newfound bouncing friend with a choke chain before he could catapult himself past me.

I wanted to dispose of him first before I dealt with Topsy and Turvey.

Dispose?

Well, I didn't mean I was going to shoot the idiot! But to be honest, it wasn't far from my mind.

The good news was, thank goodness he was clean and had not got anything on him…

Meaning cat or dog crap!

Before installing him in his run and warm sleeping quarters, clutching a powerful torch, I took bouncing Bertie the copycat kangaroo, for a short walk into the darkness of the night. The wind was howling and hurtling leaves everywhere with the hail relentlessly pelting down. It was no surprise to me that Bertie bounced all the way around the short walk just as he had been doing throughout my tortuous journey.

After his walk, I towelled him down and we finally parted company as I installed him in his heated kennel.

It was then that I realised, I was plastered in mud.

Well, I sincerely hoped it was mud!

Next, it was the turn of the poor little tabbies, Topsy and Turvey. I have to say, that after the journey, those two names are very appropriate. Please, believe me, I have not made those names up.

Again, I walked behind the Daihatsu, and for sure, I most certainly was not looking forward to the horrible sight that was surely waiting inside to greet me. Carefully I re-opened the rear door only to find that the two unfortunate cat baskets had been overturned by the bouncing idiot Bertie.

Holding my breath, I righted the baskets.

There was not a sound, within…

Gently, I lifted the first lid and peered inside…

The smell was awful…

But…

There was purring.

Well, thank goodness for that!

Ditto, it was the same with the other basket.

Unfortunately, both cats were covered in crap and pee.

At least it was a blessing in disguise, Bertie hadn't added to it!

Topsy and Turvey looked dreadful, but amazingly they meowed in a friendly way obviously asking to be let out and fussed by me. No way was I interested in cuddling and stroking them. Not only did they look awful, but they smelt awful too!

Have you ever tried bathing a cat?

I can assure you it is virtually impossible.

So, what was I going to do with them?

No way could I bathe them!

My mind was searching for a plan.

One at a time, I gently picked up Topsy and Turvey's baskets with them still inside and carried them into the grooming room where we usually bathed the dogs in the normal-sized white ceramic bath. I ran some warm water and tested the temperature with the back of my hand. Then wearing rubber gloves, I lifted them out in turn then sponged and cleaned them to the best of my ability. To my surprise, neither of them showed any sign of aggression letting me do what was necessary. And to show their trust in me, they purred even more.

I was certainly glad that I was wearing rubber gloves, but that didn't help my sensitive nostrils...

A clothes peg came to mind!

I hosed down their baskets, before gently putting them back in. Thankfully, the rain had stopped, so finally, one basket at a time, I carried them down to the cattery to install them in their nice warm beds for the night. I was quite pleased with how they looked. Although a little damp, the most important thing was, they were clean.

Cats are very clean creatures by habit and I knew that they would put any finishing touches needed to their coats themselves. The next morning, I hoped that they would look just as if nothing had ever happened to them. And the next morning, they did!

I hoped that one day, those two lovely cats would get their own back on Bertie the bouncing Beagle.

Eventually, when our business was well established, (in fact, it took off like a train). I made sure that Geoff's collection and delivery service was the first extra job of mine to get knocked on the head.

Well, well, what a surprise!

CHAPTER 12

The Decoy

An amusing short story about two dogs, (to coin a phrase) taking the pee out of me!

Two Golden Retrievers arrived on the premises and their names were Kerry and Sam.

Yet another, Sam!

Having gone through the usual routine with Kerry and Sam's owner regarding their vaccination certificates, we walked out of the office to his car containing the two Golden Retrievers. He attached the leads to their collars and out of the car the dogs jumped. Then he handed the leads to me and got back into the car to make his departure. I watched his car leave the car park and turn down the drive. As I held the leads Kerry decided to relieve herself. I stood in amazement as I watched the brown smelly stuff excrete onto my beautiful clean car park.

Of course, it would have to be the real sloppy stuff that is more difficult to clean up.

I suppose I couldn't blame her because she had just had quite a long journey. (This was when we were really established and customers were coming from all over.) It was quite a cold day in October and as I watched Kerry doing her 'business', and I seemed to be warming up quite nicely.

But not all of over my body!

I was getting quite a pleasant warm sensation down my right leg.

I looked down wondering why my leg was getting lovely and warm.

But it wasn't a lovely sight that greeted my eyes!

Sam, was looking up at me almost as if he had a grin on his face and with his leg cocked high in the air he was peeing down my jeans.

What did he think I was?

A lamppost?

I jumped back to get out of range.

But, I was far, far too late.

And to cap it all, my jeans that were clean on that morning were well and truly soaked with Sam's warm smelly gift.

How come accidents never happened to my jeans when they were in need of a change?

Do you remember what Benson did to my jeans in the first book?

Kerry's sloppy mess needed a shovel, a bucket of water, disinfectant and a long-handled scrubbing brush. I wasn't in the best of moods, (can you blame me?) when I spotted Haley walking up towards the kennel block from the cattery.

I shouted and beckoned,

"HALEY, CAN YOU COME OVER HERE PLEASE, THERE'S BEEN AN ACCIDENT."

'Oh, and get a washing machine for my jeans while you're at it!'

Haley ran up to me and my two new friends. When she saw the stinking mess on the car park she wasn't too happy, but when she saw my jeans...

She burst out laughing!

I said,

"Hey, it's not funny!"

Haley laughed more.

Then I joined in and said,

"Okay, I can see the funny side of this, with a bit of luck, next time it will be you!"

With that, I left Haley to clear up the sloppy dog poo that was bordering on diarrhoea and proceeded to walk the two otherwise lovely dogs into the woods. By this time, my previous warm sensation had turned into an unpleasantly cold one. Also, I developed a limp because I was trying to stop my leg from touching the cold wet material, meaning my jeans.

I am sure I heard sniggering and laughter from some of my staff as I started the walk around the woods. I knew from then on that I would have to watch those two devils in the future.

Or better still, get another fool to walk them!

Perhaps it was all part of Kerry and Sam's devious plan to attract my attention by using Kerry for a decoy as Sam scored a direct hit.

Now this is something I have noticed when dog owners take their dogs for a walk. They stare intensely at the dog's backside as it squats and goes to the toilet. Obviously, they are watching what is vacating from the dog's body. As they watch, they seem to have a look of intense concentration on their faces, not the dogs, I mean the owners!

I wonder what these owners are thinking, as they watch this intimate performance taking place.

Oh, that's a big one!

Or...

That wasn't as big as yesterday!

Or...

I like the colour of that one!

Well, I most certainly did not study what type of crap Kerry had deposited on my car park!

CHAPTER 13

A Great Big Fat Cat!

This is a short story about a cat and a very, very big one at that!

So here we go.

Fat Cat was his name and he certainly deserved it.

He was enormous! Quite easily the biggest cat that we had ever seen.

The question was...

How did his owners know he was going to be big and fat before he grew to his full size? Perhaps he was a very fat kitten or maybe they changed his name when they could see how big and fat he was getting. Strangely, I never thought to ask. Anyway, when Fat Cat stayed with us he was certainly fat all right. According to his owner, he weighed in at 33 lbs, almost 15 kg.

My Goodness!

Yes, almost 15 kilos of pure feline bulk!

And that, my readers, is a very, very big cat.

It was a good job Fat Cat was a good-natured character because if he wasn't, we would have certainly had our hands full.

Hands full. We had a devil of a job to pick him up!

Fat Cat was so big that he couldn't even get up the ladder to his sleeping box which was only thirty inches off the tiled floor. The following photo is of our very first guests in the cattery showing the ladders before I painted them white. I must add, that all the other cats that stayed with us had no problem. Even if our fat friend could have achieved the climb, he would not have fitted through the entrance of the sleeping box. So we had to put a special box on the tiled floor for him.

Here are our very first guests relaxing in the new cattery

Mr Leyton, who was Fat Cat's owner, was a tall strong-looking man. It was usually him who carried the heavy cat to and from the cattery if

I was not around. For sure, Fat Cat was far too heavy for any of the girls, especially when he was inside his homemade wooden carrying box.

In fact, two girls would not have managed him.

A wheelbarrow did come to mind!

Mr Leyton made Fat Cat's wooden container because he could not find a pet shop that stocked one big enough. After a few visits to our premises, I advised him to drive his car down to the cattery to save him or me hauling the big cat the one hundred yards or so from the car park to the cattery building.

According to Mr Leyton, when Fat Cat was targeted and charged by a dog, he never bothered to run away. Perhaps he was just far too fat to run. The canine tribe must have thought that he was rather big because when they charged him at speed, he just stood his ground. That is when the A. B. S. (Anti-locking, Braking System) came into play as the dog skidded to a halt in a cloud of dust. Then in total disarray, after a glare and a swipe from a large paw, the dog beat a hasty retreat in the opposite direction with its tail between its legs. I think if I was a dog, I would have done the same!

There is nothing else to say about this lovable fat character, except myself and all the staff, were very, very fond of him and I just had to include him in this book.

Cats and weight

Domestic cats usually weigh between 8 lbs to 11 lbs (3.6 kg) to (5 kg). Meow, a cat from America at the time of his death was the heaviest cat in the world and weighed close to 40 lbs, (18 kg) which is almost four times more than the regular size of a cat. Himmy, a cat from Australia holds the world record and weighed in at 47 lbs (21.3 kg).

Himmy the holder of the Guinness Book of Records heaviest cat in the world

A cat's weight can depend on the breed and frame. For example, a Siamese cat weighs around 5 lbs, (2.268 kg) while Maine Coon cats can weigh 25 lbs (11.3 kg).

Well, Fat Cat was fat, but I have to say, nothing like the size of Himmy.

CHAPTER 14

Tango and the Foxtrot!

MICK

Young kids and their pets.

This is a very short story that I couldn't resist adding to this book.

It is about a small female cat called Tango and a lovable dog called Basil. Incidentally, Basil looked very much like a fox. Hence, his name copied from a popular children's TV program, Basil Brush.

We have two very good friends Geoff and Janina who owned Tango and Basil. Tango was a small tortoiseshell with beautiful markings. Their daughter Olivia and son Julian who were very young when this story took place could do absolutely anything they liked with the pair.

One day, we arrived at Geoff and Janina's house and could not believe our eyes at the wonderful sight that greeted us…

Tango was sitting in the utility sink which was half full of water and Olivia was massaging shampoo into her coat. This procedure was followed by Olivia pouring warm water over the purring cat. Afterwards, she towelled Tango down and then sat her on her knee as she blow-dried her with a powerful hair drier. The cat was purring and obviously enjoying the attention.

We were astounded because everybody knows that cats generally hate water. Normally it is impossible to bath cats unless you sedate them. For sure, it was something that we would never attempt in our business. I think most of our feline guests would have torn us to shreds.

Now it is Basil's turn...

On another day that we visited the family, Olivia dressed Basil in doll's clothing and put sunglasses on him. Then she put him in a doll's pram and pushed him around the garden.

Her brother Julian followed with Tango on a lead. Attached to the pink coat that Tango was wearing were clothes pegs, with ribbons and bells that jangled as they walked behind Basil's pram.

A truly delightful sight.

Both animals used our facilities on regular occasions and I have to say, that if all the pets that came to us had Tango's and Basil's temperament, it would have made our job…

An absolute doddle!

CHAPTER 15

Car Park Capers

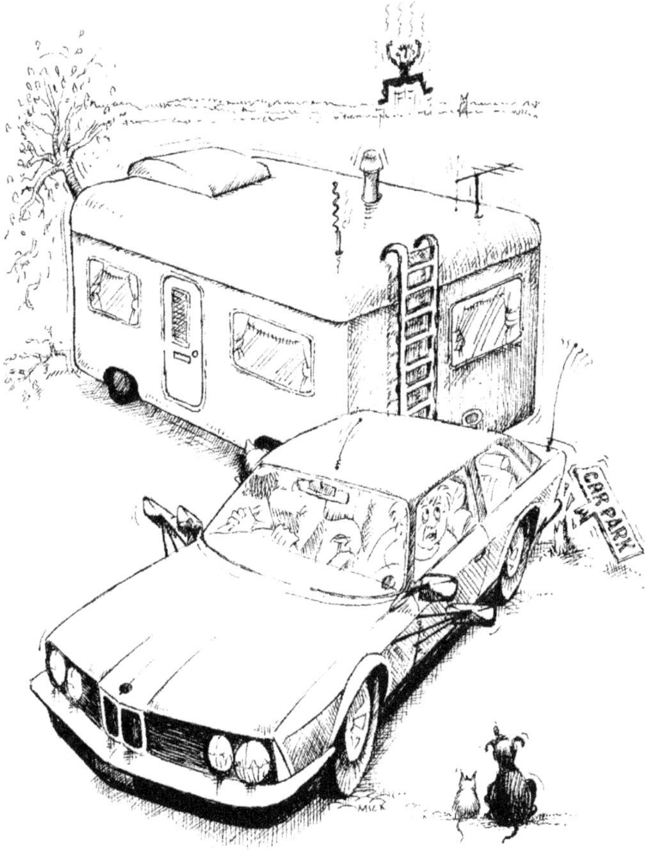

Four amusing stories.

I have often pondered…

Who are the best drivers, ladies or gentlemen?

Now that is a leading question which is often asked by many people of both sexes.

Well, in my opinion, I would say that men are far more aggressive drivers than ladies. Also, I think that the fairer sex, unlike their macho counterparts, are generally more careful and observant. (Could this be Geoff creeping here?) Of course, we all have different opinions on this subject.

But which of the sexes are best at parking a car?

Or, should I say reversing?

Now that is a very good question!

Story Number 1 - Mount Everest

This first story takes place in the very early days of our business and is about a lady parking her car. And with me being a gentleman, I mean it's only fair ladies should be checked out first.

This incident took place in January on our very new unfinished car park that could take twenty cars at a push and that's not including the grassed area with the sign...

PLEASE KEEP OFF THE GRASS.

Unfortunately, a few drivers ignored that sign!

The lady in question was a friend of ours named Gill who had a lovely Border Collie called Sam.

As I have mentioned many times before, Sam seemed to be the most popular name for male dogs, especially Border Collies.

Do you remember in one of my earlier stories when the wrong Sam was delivered to the wrong home?

Anyway, I'm not going to embarrass Gill by giving away her surname. The embarrassing thing for this particular lady was the predicament she got herself into when she was parking her car.

I have never seen anything quite like it, before or since!

The time of day is quite crucial to this story. With it being mid-winter, it was almost dark. It was 5 p.m. which just happened to be our closing time. Gill's car was one of two on the car park, the other belonged to our very first manager, Clare.

So why should it be so difficult to park a car on a car park that was virtually empty with loads and loads of space?

Well, not quite as much space as a Tesco car park, but Gill certainly had plenty of room to manoeuvre. I have to admit that she did park it on her first attempt. But that was not the problem. Yes, it is okay to park a car, but eventually, you do have to drive it away again even though you might have completed the first task successfully.

But, why did she park her car in such a unique

way?

Here comes the answer...

Sitting in my office with a full view of the car park, I checked Sam's vaccination certificate. I handed it back to Gill who left the office and walked to her car to fetch Sam. She brought him back on his lead right in front of the office where she handed him over to Clare and said goodbye to me. So, off Clare and Sam went for his introductory walk around our woodland circuit. I was checking the number of spring bookings in the kennel's diary when I heard Gill's car door slam and her car start up.

I thought no more of it and carried on thumbing through the diary.

I knew there was something amiss when I heard a car engine revving or should I say screaming at ten thousand revs a minute.

'That car engine sounds really loud. What on earth is this all about?'

Hearing the racket, I looked through the office window, and the light had faded to pitch black, but I could still make out a car which was on the other side of Clare's car about fifteen yards away.

The only car it could be would be Gill's...

And sure enough, it was!

Clare, having installed Sam into his quarters, walked into the office.

She said,

"You won't believe what that lady’s gone and done."

When people say in a statement to me such as,

"You won't believe!"

I think,

‘UGH, UGH, trouble ahead.'

And I'm usually right!

THIS TURNED OUT TO BE TROUBLE, WITH A CAPITAL…T!!!

Puzzled, I walked out to Gill's car which should have left a while ago and I could see Gill behind the wheel revving the engine like blue murder.

But the car was not going anywhere.

Any time soon!

'Whatever is the problem? Can't she get it in gear?'

Oh yes, it was in gear alright...

Gill's car was a front-wheeled drive Volkswagen Golf and the front wheels were spinning, not on 'Terra Firma,' but unbelievingly in the air at seemingly a hundred miles an hour.

And that is no exaggeration!

And there was never going to be any movement either because the two front driving wheels were a foot off the ground.

Gill was revving her poor car so hard, it sounded louder than the start of a Formula One race.

It would not have made the slightest bit of difference if the car had got four-wheel drive because the back wheels were also a foot off the ground. Her car was in a similar situation to a plane taking off or landing.

So how on earth had she done it?

Well, the lovely lady had only driven onto the top of a pile of stone chippings. The chippings were waiting for me to rake and spread them over our not-quite-completed car park the following morning.

Boy, was I going to have a job spreading that lot about with a car perched on the summit of our own mini-Mount Everest.

'Why on earth has she driven up there?'

I suppose the usual answer that mountaineers give will suffice...

"Because it is there!!!"

It was there alright, and 'Muggins' here was going to be the one who had to shift it.

I walked up to Gill's car, which was still revving up rather enthusiastically. I tapped on her window and even as the window slid down she continued revving the unfortunate little car.

Gill, our lady Grand Prix driver issued a statement that I will remember for the rest of my days!

She said,

"The car doesn't seem to be moving, yet the speedometer is reading twenty-five miles an hour!"

'What???'

Now, how was I supposed to reply to a statement like that?

Momentarily, I was speechless.

I didn't know whether to laugh or cry.

Being the happy chappy I am, I chose the former.

I asked Gill very politely or should I say, I yelled to make myself heard above the din,

"CAN YOU STOP REVVING THE ENGINE AND SWITCH IT OFF PLEASE?"

And she did. Thank goodness for that.

I could have easily dragged her car off the summit of mini-Everest with my 4 x 4 Jeep, but I was afraid I might damage her car.

I decided to do things the safest way which is very often the hardest way.

Sam was only boarding with us for two days and if I had not come to the rescue, Gill's car might well have been stuck there for the duration of his stay. It was well and truly dark when I hacked away at Gill's mini-Everest with a shovel and rake.

It took me the best part of an hour to clear away the chippings from under her car without damaging it. Eventually, after my toiling and sweating (in January) the Volkswagen finally touched down unscathed.

As Gill watched me wipe my sweating brow with a big white handkerchief, meekly she asked,

"Shall I drive it out now?"

'There's absolutely no way you are getting in that driver's seat young lady!'

I replied,

"No, don't worry, I'll drive it out for you."

I could just imagine her getting it stuck again

and me being there for another hour.

So, without taking any chances, I drove it out.

Having rescued the car safely off the mountain of chippings which by then looked more like a volcano with a crater in the middle, I handed her back the keys and waved goodbye.

I went to bed that night, a lot more tired than I previously envisaged and was still extremely puzzled. Why hadn't she seen that mound of chippings? And if she had, why on earth did she drive her car onto it?

Possibly, her excuse might have been...

Well, it was **dark**!

Story Number 2 – A Man And His Caravan

So, now it is the turn of the first gentleman driver in our battle of the sexes. Okay ladies, you can rub your hands together, for sure, you are really going to enjoy this one.

This story took place in the latter years when the business had really taken off.

This gentleman phoned me before he came to collect his cat on a very busy Saturday afternoon in August. On Saturdays we had lots and lots of deliveries and collections, in fact, this particular day was an exceptionally busy one, with cats, dogs and customers coming and going all day long. Rather than reveal the name of the cat and caravan owner, to save him any embarrassment, I will call him George.

George rang me up because he wanted to come and pick his cat up with his caravan still in tow.

He asked,

"Have you room to turn a caravan around on your premises? It would save me a lot of time rather than going home first to uncouple it."

After the previous experience with the lady on mini–Mount Everest, I hoped he meant to turn it around and not turn it over.

"How big is it?"

"Oh, it's just average-sized."

'Now, what does that mean? Just average-sized?'

I had visions of a caravan, as long as an articulated truck appearing and ending up going across my beautiful grass.

Politely I asked,

"Are you used to reversing it?"

"If you have plenty of room, I will have no problem at all."

With it being such a busy day and me not having a lot of time to think about it, I took the risk and said yes.

Anyway, on more than one occasion in the days of building the pet hotel, I had witnessed skillful gentleman drivers, (sorry ladies) reversing low loaders bearing giant mechanical diggers into the same area where George would be manoeuvring his hopefully average-sized caravan.

So, why worry?

What could possibly go wrong?

I put the thoughts of caravans and low-loaders to the back of my mind and continued dealing with the numerous customers who were delivering and collecting their pets.

Half an hour or so later the man with the caravan turned up along with his wife and walked into the office.

I stood up with a dreaded thought in my mind.

'How big is the caravan?'

I looked across the busy car park looking for a potential problem.

Problem?

Now you're expecting something really big.

Aren't you?

You're expecting me to say,

“It was absolutely enormous!”

Well wrong, it was thankfully just a normal run-of-the-mill caravan that we see on the roads all the time.

George paid his bill and one of the staff handed his wife the beige plastic carrier containing their cat.

As they turned to leave, I politely asked,

"Can you manage to back the caravan out alright?"

"Oh yes, thanks. I can see there's plenty of room. See you next time."

"Ok, thank you so much. Bye-bye."

‘What a nice couple.’

But, was it, bye-bye?

So, as far as I was concerned, that potential problem was well out of the way, so I got back to dealing with the continuous flow of pets and customers and thought nothing more about men with caravans.

Cars were coming and going in and out of the car park at a fair rate of knots and everything was running smoothly. Just like clockwork.

Dare I say I was having a really good day?

There had been so many people in the office that I hadn't even had time to look up, let alone look out the window.

Then I heard a female voice from the back of the queuing customers shout,

"MR DOODY. THERE'S A GUY OUT THERE HAVING TROUBLE WITH A CARAVAN!"

'Oh no, not two caravans in one day!'

'I bet this is the giant one I've been dreading.'

'Why haven't I been warned about this second one?'

But to my surprise, it wasn't a second one.

It was George!

'Oh no!'

He was still here and I had dealt with him well over half an hour ago.

'What was he doing?'

I asked Kathy to take over the busy desk.

I marched briskly across to a BMW coupled to a caravan and couldn't believe what I was looking at…

'Oh no!'

The car and caravan were jackknifed right up against our boundary fence alongside the private drive that led to our cottage.

Jackknifed?

Jackknifed was putting it mildly!

The car and caravan were almost parallel to each other.

'Arghhh, I don't need this today of all days!'

Now, not blowing my trumpet too much, I have been backing trailers from the age of thirteen, either with tractors or Land Rovers, varying from two wheels to six wheels and I must say I was quite proficient. But the position or should I say predicament that George had manoeuvred his car and caravan in made me scratch my head. Maybe I could have got them out, but there was absolutely no way he was going to achieve it. If he carried on the way he was going, it would take a crane to solve the problem.

Politely I said,

"I see you have a slight problem with the caravan. I'm quite used to reversing trailers. Would you like me to have a go?"

George who had gone red in the face, replied,

"Don't worry; I'll have it out in a jiffy."

Was he joking, or what?

Never in a month of Sundays was he ever going to get that car and caravan out of there.

I could see that he was turning the steering wheel the wrong way.

George's wife firmly piped up,

"Why don't you let Mr Doody help you."

Like a little lamb, our George, the red-faced embarrassed driver gave up the ghost and resignedly gave up his seat.

So, with Mrs George sitting in the front passenger seat, I got behind the wheel. I was about to start the complicated process of shunting the car out of its unbelievable predicament when I heard Kathy shout,

"GEOFF, THERE IS A LADY ON THE PHONE FOR YOU."

"TELL HER, I'LL CALL BACK IN A FEW MINUTES."

"I'M SORRY, BUT SHE SAYS SHE MUST SPEAK TO YOU NOW... AND IT'S VERY URGENT."

'Oh no! Of all times, please not now!'

I jumped out of George's car, making sure that I took his car keys with me. I certainly wasn't going to let him have another attempt at making things even worse.

I ran across the car park to get to the phone.

Was it urgent?

Of course, it wasn't!

It was Mrs Midgley, a lovely old lady who always asked to speak to me, and yes, of course, it could have waited, but the customer always comes first.

Mrs Midgley had a slight problem with Sophie, her cat, she had collected her a couple of days ago. She needed reassurance from me regarding worming tablets prescribed by the vet. She obviously preferred me to her vet! Politely, I advised her that all cats needed worming periodically and to follow the vet's instructions carefully.

Obviously thinking that I had got all the time in the world she said,

"Oh, while I'm speaking to you Mr Doody, can I book Sophie in for a two-week stay in October please?"

I was thinking that I should be passing this phone over to Kathy, but I could see she was up to her neck with cats, dogs and customers. Also, our staff were run off their feet carrying incoming cats to the cattery, installing outgoing cats into their carriers, walking incoming dogs and handing over the dogs that were leaving.

The lovely lady on the other end of the line had been using us with her lovely cat Sophie from the very start of our business and she always liked to deal with the nice Mr Doody.

With forced patience, I took the booking dates from her as she fondly talked about Sophie. She wasn't to know I was just a little bit busy. I didn't know which way to turn and I had a man with a caravan waiting patiently for me or at least, I hoped he was waiting patiently. Anyway, George couldn't worsen the situation because...

HA! HA!

I had his car keys!

Eventually, I got back to red-faced George, who was strutting up and down along the side of his stranded boy's toys with a puzzled expression on his face.

I got back into his driver's seat and studied the situation. The front bumper of the BMW was within inches of our rabbit netting boundary fence and there was absolutely no room to manoeuvre. Red-faced George had done an excellent job that needed to be seen to be believed. I tried a couple of small manoeuvres, but it wasn't many seconds before I realised that the only way out of this mess was to cut the fence.

My new rabbit-proof wire netting fence!!!

'Arghhh! I don't believe this! It's less than a year old.'

I ran the hundred and fifty yards to our garage, picked up my trusty wire cutters and then ran all the way back. Sweating and gasping for breath with the wire cutters in my hand I attacked the fence that was still shiny with newness. Once the fence was down it still took me a good five minutes of shunting backwards and forwards to eventually point George's BMW with caravan in a homeward direction.

It was two hours after their initial arrival that George, his wife, cat, car and caravan left our premises. Hopefully, the next time their cat boarded with us George would not be in such a rush to pick it up and go home first to dump the caravan.

So, who is the winner so far?

The ladies or the gentlemen?

Story Number 3 - A Lady And Her Trailer

I have one more amusing story about a lady driver. I witnessed this amusing event from the sanctuary of our cottage. At that time, both my feet were in plaster because I was recovering from a double bunion operation and was bored out of my mind by the enforced inactivity. Little did I know that in the next few minutes, my boredom was going to get some amusing relief. I had been in plaster for three weeks, so I filled in my time by taking bookings using my sales pitch on the phone and entering the dates in our diaries. A red diary for cats and blue for dogs.

I had been sitting in my captains chair, (a hardwood padded leather armchair on casters with a low curved back, supported by spindles) for a couple of hours and felt like stretching. I stood up and stretched my arms above my head. As I did so, I looked out of the study window across the lawned area towards the car park.

A lady driver was attempting to reverse a car coupled to a small tent trailer. She was on our drive and it was obvious to me, she wanted to back her car and trailer onto the carpark.

As the lady attempted the manoeuvre, I could see that trouble was brewing. Without a doubt, the trailer was not going in the direction that she intended. Any time soon!

The car and trailer jack-knifed to the right, so she drove the car forward and tried reversing again. This second attempt resulted in a jackknife to the left. So, after numerous unfruitful attempts, it was quite obvious that she wasn't going to back the trailer in any direction. Let alone the correct one! She had plenty of room on the car park because there was only one car on it which belonged to Pat, my manager.

After the lady driver's fruitless attempts, Pat walked over to offer some assistance. With a smile on my face the next thing I observed, was Pat sitting in the driver's seat. Then Pat had a few attempts to reverse the trailer and was just as unsuccessful as her predecessor. By then I was getting quite amused with all this entertainment and my boredom had waned rapidly. My curiosity grew even more when I watched Pat go inside the kennel block and reappear with two young members of staff.

'Now what are they going to do? Those two girls haven't even learnt to drive yet!'

I admired Pat's initiative as the little trailer was uncoupled from the car, and then the four ladies pushed it into the car park. I realised that their plan was to enable the lady driver to reverse her trailer-less car onto the car park to the waiting trailer.

In reverse, the car went, but my lady entertainer could not keep it in a straight line as she tried to back it to the trailer. She was all over the place. So, she stopped and got out of her car. The next amazing thing that happened was the four ladies pushed and manoeuvred the trailer into position and recoupled it to her car.

Well, I suppose, that was one way to reverse a trailer!

What I really wanted to know is, how on earth was our lady driver going to manage when she finally reached her planned destination? She was alone and would not have the help from our staff!

So, is it true what they say about lady drivers not being able to reverse?

Story Number 4 – About Me!

My friends have often praised me by saying, I am a good driver.

I bet you ladies are thinking.

'Yes, you would be, wouldn't you?'

I love driving and passed my test first time only seven weeks after my seventeenth birthday. (Geoff is really bragging now!) Even now, every time I drive, I consider it a challenge and give every trip however short, my utmost concentration. Driving, as far as I am concerned, is all about concentration and anticipation. Now, after all that waffling, the ladies are really going to like this story.

At the end of our long private drive on the right-hand side just before it joined the A 41 highway was a clear area of woodland. In the clearance stood three large commercial green wheelie bins.

They were for our exclusive use and twice a week I went down the drive in my brand-new silver Toyota Land Cruiser to take rubbish to those bins. (Yes, I had come up in the world since my Daihatsu Jeep.)

I was towing a trailer fully loaded with black bin bags. The bags contained empty cans, cat litter and all sorts of general rubbish from the business. With my rubber-gloved hands, it took me at least twenty minutes to load the smelly bags onto the trailer and then another twenty minutes to offload them into the wheelie bins. Rubber gloves were a must because I did not want any unpleasant smells on my hands, meaning cat poo or pee.

I have to say, it was not one of my most pleasant tasks.

At that time, we were planning to have the tarmac access widened enabling two cars to pass each other. The reason being, a car could be waiting to drive out onto the busy highway, whilst another car could be waiting on the highway to turn in, so this made it potentially dangerous.

On this particular day, after offloading the trailer, in deep thought I stared at the drive entrance planning how the job would be tackled. Still contemplating, I jumped back into my big new shiny machine. I turned the ignition key and drove forward twenty yards or so. I sat there for about five minutes figuring out how much work would be involved and more to the point. How much was it going to cost?

My mind was miles away from my next job which was to reverse and make a three-point turn which would point me or should I say, my shiny new toy in the correct direction to proceed back up the drive.

Without turning around to look where I was going, I engaged reverse gear and then half flattened the accelerator as I confidently turned the steering wheel enabling me to reverse to my right where there was plenty of space.

Suddenly...

BANG!!!

Instantly, I hit the brakes.

'OH! NO! WHAT WAS THAT?'

I looked into my driver's side mirror...

To my horror, I just could not believe what I was seeing!

I had totally forgotten I was towing the trailer!

'WHAT!'

And there it was, jackknifed up along the side of my beloved brand-new Land Cruiser.

'OH! NO! NO! NO!!!'

I shot out of my wounded vehicle to inspect how much damage I had inflicted on my poor shiny toy. Luckily, it wasn't as bad as it first looked. The badly gouged rear plastic wheel arch was hanging off, but to my relief, there was no actual damage to the main bodywork. It appeared that all I needed to do was to clip the moulded wheel arch back onto the exposed plastic studs where it had been attached only seconds before. So, I attempted to press the big piece of plastic moulding back into its former position...

But it was having none of it!

No way!!!

No way was it going back on because some of the

clips were broken.

I decided the only thing to do was pull it off, but it wasn't having any of that either.

After numerous attempts, I lost my temper good and proper and kicked the stupid thing off!

All I can say is, without the moulding, it didn't half spoil the good looks of my unfortunate new vehicle.

Eventually, when I arrived back at our cottage with my tail between my legs, I phoned the Toyota garage, which was located in Stoke-on-Trent from where I purchased the Land Cruiser. I made an appointment to drive my wounded new toy over to get an estimate of the cost to repair the damage that I had inflicted.

The engineer estimated my bill to be around eight hundred pounds.

'ARGHHH!!!'

YES, EIGHT HUNDRED POUNDS!!!

A lot of money in those days!

That was certainly going to increase the price of

having the drive widened. That's for sure!

Toyota had to order the part. So, in the meantime, I had to drive the shiny new love of my life around for four weeks minus one rear offside wheel arch that was advertising for all to see, my bad driving and embarrassment.

Eventually, I did and still do see the funny side of my minor accident.

What idiot would forget he was towing a trailer when only five minutes ago he had unloaded it?

Well, I'm afraid I have to admit to that one.

Of course, a lady would never make such a silly mistake like that.

Would she?

So, perhaps I have let you guys down by being the biggest 'Wally' of all!

I bet my bottom dollar that you ladies loved that last story!

CHAPTER 16

Essential Reading

A WARNING!

Anyone wishing to run a pet hotel may change their mind after reading the following chapter after this one.

There is a widely used four-letter swear word which begins with an S and ends with a T. That swear word relates to the next two chapters very much, so as not to offend anyone, I have used the word, crap!

When running a large pet hotel for cats and dogs, unfortunately, it was a fact of life that we had to deal with loads of excrement and I mean loads of the stinking stuff.

In other words, it was just plain crap.

I suppose crap and manure can be classed as the same thing.

Interesting facts about manure

In the 16th and 17th centuries, everything had to be transported by ship. Also, it was before the invention of commercial fertilisers, so that large shipments of manure were quite common. It was shipped dry because in dry form it weighed a lot less than if it was wet. But once water (at sea) hit it, not only did it become heavier, the process of fermentation began again, of which a by-product is methane gas. As the stuff was stored below decks in bundles, you can see what could (and did) happen. Methane began to build up below decks and the first time someone came below at night with a lantern...

BOOOOM!

Several ships were destroyed in this manner before it was determined just what was causing the problem. After a few disasters, the bundles of manure were always stamped with the instruction 'Stow high in transit', which meant for the sailors to stow it high enough off the lower decks so that any water that came into the hold would not touch this volatile cargo and start the production of methane.

Thus evolved the term 'S.H.I.T', (Stow High In Transit), which has come down through the centuries and is in use to this very day. You probably did not know the true history of this word.

Well, my head is full of interesting facts and crap.

Anyway, my information about 'S.H.I.T', (Stow High In Transit), is not true. It is just one of my jokes!

I just thought I would get you going with my warped sense of humour.

Ok, let's analyse the word, crap.

A lot of folks think that the word crap derives from Thomas Crapper, a London plumber born in 1836 and died in 1910.

WRONG!

The name Crapper is a northern form of Cropper, (attested from 1221) an occupational surname obviously, but the exact reference is unclear.

So, crap has nothing to do with our friend Thomas Crapper.

But this following chapter, Dinner Talk has everything to do with crap.

Well, that's enough of all that factual crap and trivia.

Now we get to the REAL DEAL, the next chapter, which is the TRUE crap chapter.

IF YOU ARE ONE OF THE BRAVE AND NOT AT ALL SQUEAMISH...

READ ON...

CHAPTER 17

Dinner Talk

In this chapter, there are eleven very different stories.

By the way, that is not me in the rowing boat!

There is some humour in the following stories, but my advice is…

Be very selective!

ONLY THE BRAVE WILL READ THEM ALL!

This chapter contains stories that are funny, some not quite so funny, and one that is absolutely shocking, but they all revolve around that unavoidable act of nature…

Crapping!

WARNING!

SOME OF THESE STORIES SHOULD HAVE A GOVERNMENT HEALTH WARNING!

IT MIGHT BE STRONGLY ADVISABLE TO SKIP THIS CHAPTER!

ESPECIALLY IF YOU HAVE A QUEASY STOMACH!

So, here we go…

In the United Kingdom, most people have their

main meal in the evening and usually, they call it dinner. As they eat their meal various conversations may take place. The number one conversation that people often discuss is about the weather, probably because in the UK the weather can be so varied and unpredictable. Perhaps, after the weather has been discussed they might talk about their work. Or maybe their journey home.

Now I am going to inform you what we talked about in our household.

At least eighty per cent of the time we talked about excrement. Yes, we talked about crap. To be precise, cat and dog crap, even though we were eating. To us, crap was a fact of life. Crap was something we had to deal with every day of our working lives, seven days a week, week in and week out. You could say that we were crap experts.

The plain truth is, we made money from shovelling up the multi-coloured sticky stuff.

Some crap was the colour of gold.

Which was very appropriate.

Well, you know the old saying.

'Where there's muck, there's money'.

So, over the years we had become an authority on crap.

Especially cat and dog crap!

I have experienced a lot of crap in my time and I do mean the excrement type. And because of my occasional warped sense of humour, I have made a list...

A list starting with the nicer varieties of crap.

At the top of my list is a small brown bird called a sparrow. Probably because sparrow crap is so tiny. I mean you wouldn't want a flying horse or cow to crap on your head.

Would you?

Now what about swans? They fly and their crap is similar to cows. Having said that, thank goodness cows cannot fly.

Swans come in pairs because they mate for life. The male swan is called a Cob and the female, is a Pen.

Have you ever been in a rowing boat when a pair of swans decide to take off in your direction?

WELL, I HAVE!

For sure, it is an absolute certainty that they will head for your boat as they struggle to get airborne. When swans take off, their massive wings beat the water into a froth. Their large black webbed feet, known as paddles trail the water. So, when they have achieved lift-off. What do they do next? Well, they release half a bucket full of sloppy green crap that hurtles towards your boat. The crap splatters across the water, not unlike machine gun bullets. If you are fortunate, the flying crap stops just short of your boat. But if you are unfortunate, as I have been, you will get splattered maybe thinking a flying cow has flown over.

Swans eat grass just like cows so their crap is of a similar green sloppy consistency.

Kathy loves horses and has owned quite a few, therefore we have shovelled up plenty of horse crap in our time.

In the horsey world of racing, there is a well-known saying...

'You put money in one end, and out of the other end comes crap'.

Money paid for horse food is turned into horse crap and a mountainous amount is produced. Well, at least we did get our money's worth. Every day, we had enough horse crap to fill a half-wheelbarrow, and as a bonus, we could spread it around our garden. I am sure that keen gardeners know that roses love it.

Now I certainly would not fancy spreading cat and dog crap around the garden. It doesn't bear thinking about. In my opinion, horse crap is probably the second nicest crap I have ever had the pleasure to meet, probably due to the subtle smell and it doesn't stick to your hands.

Okay, let's get back to our main subject, cat and dog crap.

Comparing the two I would say that cat crap is a clear winner in nicety over dog crap, that is providing you don't get your nose too close. Cat turds are usually much smaller than dog turds and they all seem to come in a standard size. Cat turds are usually firmer than dog turds, especially if their main diet is dried food. Generally, fishy or meaty tinned food has a potent smell even before it has been processed by our furry feline friend into a neat turd with a pointed end.

Or something much sloppier.

Yuk!

Fortunately, most of the cats that boarded with us used their litter trays and the cat turds were a light greyish colour similar to the vulpine family of foxes. The nice thing about cats compared to dogs is, at least they have etiquette. I don't know who taught them to do it, but at least they bury their crap.

We all know dogs have no interest in burying their crap.

Hands up, who has put their foot on and skidded in dog crap on the pavement?

In my opinion, dog crap is the second-nastiest crap on the planet.

Coming in first is the human stuff.

Thank goodness we didn't have to deal with that variety of crap.

Dog crap can be quite disgusting and comes in all shapes, sizes, colours and smells. The fresh glistening brown turds seem to smell the worst and supposedly come from a healthy dog. Well, what about a dog with an upset stomach?

I will ease myself around the word diarrhoea for the time being.

WARNING!

All this nonsense is just a build-up, to what is to follow...

So, this is the point where I talk about a few dogs that produced all this money-making crap.

Now, is definitely the time to miss this chapter if you have a queasy stomach!

DON'T SAY I DIDN'T WARN YOU!

So, here we go...

Actually, the first story I have chosen is more humorous than shocking because I thought it best to ease you in gently...

Henry

This is a story about a Bulldog guest who visited us on a regular basis. This particular Bulldog did not have a name relating to Sir Winston Churchill like most did. His name was Henry. Perhaps he was named after one of the English Kings. I have to say that Henry produced some very fine turds in his time. In fact, they were turds to be proud of.

I mean Henry the dog, not Henry the King!

Henry's turds were always perfectly formed and very easy to shovel up. If you were an expert at crap shovelling like my good self, more often than not it was scooped up without a trace of it ever existing. But if you were a beginner, you could often leave a heavy skid mark on the concrete floor of the run.

Before we really got to know Henry, he was a bit of 'A pain in the ass'.

Whoops! Sorry!

I meant a pain in the backside!

As soon as Henry proudly produced an immaculate turd, he started yapping and this could go on for a good ten minutes. Besides, the noise getting on our nerves, I thought I saw some of our other canine guests cover their ears with their paws!

If they could have talked, I am sure they would have shouted out,

"Can someone tell that noisy pratt to be quiet?"

Well, we used to tell Henry to be quiet all the time, but it just didn't seem to make the slightest bit of difference.

So, what was the cure for Henry's exuberant yapping?

I decided to have a word with Henry's owners on the day that they collected him. I wanted to find out if they knew what caused Henry's annoying habit.

Take note, I am not giving away the name of Henry's owners.

So, here are the words that Henry's male owner used,

"Oh, sorry, we forgot to tell you about that one!"

'They always do. Don't they?'

"If you give Henry biscuits after he has done his 'business', he will instantly shut up. But he must have three biscuits because he can count you know."

'Is this guy crazy, or what?'

Anyway, like the good proprietor I was, I wrote on Henry's information sheet.

HENRY MUST HAVE THREE BISCUITS AFTER HE HAS DONE HIS BUSINESS, THIS CLEVER CHAPPY CAN COUNT UP TO THREE. HA! HA! HA!

So, with this enlightening exciting new information, it enabled us to write it on his card the next time he boarded with us.

On Henry's following visit, we wrote the instructions about his three biscuits on his blue card which was attached to the outside of the mesh gate to his run. After all, it was a bit important.

Especially for our long-suffering ears! Not counting our other canine guests!

Henry for some reason never had a crap when we took him for a walk. Perhaps he was just too shy to do his 'business' in front of anyone or maybe the devious old devil just wanted some biscuits. Who knows? Anyway, as soon as Henry was put back into his run after the walk...

Inevitably the yapping started.

One of the girls shouted,

"HENRY'S HAD A CRAP. HAS ANYONE SEEN GEOFF? HE WANTS TO BE THE FIRST TO TAKE HIM HIS THREE BISCUITS!"

Yes, yes, yes!

I had already informed the staff that I wanted to be the first person to witness this rare occurrence. So, on hearing this exciting news, I hurtled towards Henry's kennel. I was carrying a large yellow bucket and a short-handled shovel in my left hand and three of Henry's favourite biscuits in my right. This was in mounting anticipation of whether Henry could count or not.

For sure, I was going to be the first one to test him.

I walked into the yapping Bulldog's run and offered him one biscuit.

Greedily, he snatched it from my hand.

YAP! YAP! YAP!

Biscuit number two was swallowed, almost taking my hand with it.

YAP! YAP! YAP!

Biscuit number three, CRUNCH! CRUNCH! CRUNCH! Disappeared down his cavernous throat.

Followed by, complete and utter silence...

'My goodness! It worked!'

With that, Henry, wagging his stumpy tail turned his back on me and sauntered away to disappear into his sleeping quarters.

So, after his reward, the old boy went for a

snooze.

Was Henry, this noble dog intelligent? Or what?

Not only could Henry count, he even wanted a reward for letting us know that his run wanted cleaning.

'Sweet dreams Henry.'

I could not believe that we had suffered Henry's barking for so long when he boarded with us the first time. And just because his owners had never thought to tell us that all Henry wanted was his three biscuits for being a good boy by letting us know that he had done his 'business' and it needed clearing up.

Henry was very happy with his three biscuits and so were we. Especially with the welcoming sound of silence.

Well, what a lovely ending to that crap story.

Make the most of that little tale, because things are going to get worse...

MUCH, MUCH...

WORSE!!!

Cats

Generally, cats are clean creatures, but we met a few that were not. Normally, cats are meticulous in keeping themselves clean and spend hours looking after their glossy coats. When a cat cleans itself, it is an art in itself. With a back leg pointing vertically in the air, it licks furiously with that tiny pink rough tongue.

Cats usually bury their excrement, or should I say crap. Hey, and more often than not, in someone else's garden. They never seem to crap on their own doorstep.

When two or three cats from the same household were boarding in one run, we provided separate litter trays. We did this because they would not use the same litter tray as their companions. It was probably a territorial trait. Or perhaps they wanted their own private loo.

Quite often, we found that cat owners with more than one cat did not want them separated. They said it was because they couldn't live apart, but I think the main reason was the discount we offered for cats sharing. It was total overcrowding in some cases, but we always had to do as the customer instructed, because here we go again...

The customer is always right.

Generally, for cat litter, we used wood shavings that came in large compressed bales, but with long-haired cats shavings could tangle in their fur so we used pellets that were quite expensive. Occasionally, we had a fussy cat that would not use the litter tray that we had provided.

One particular tom cat was quite unique when he came to burying his crap.

Where do you think he buried it?

Well, in his bedding of course!

And not only crap. Far too often, he peed in there as well. I mean, where else would the joker hide his crap? Other than in his bed! I suppose it seemed a pretty obvious option to the cat.

What a lovely experience it was to be greeted first thing in the morning having just eaten a nice breakfast, with that feline present expertly wrapped up like a Christmas present in the bedding.

Well, at least it had tried to bury it!

Cat bedding was usually provided by the owners. Often, it was an old woollen jumper or something similar which had the owner's scent on it. The idea of cat owners bringing something personal was strongly recommended because it would remind the cat of home sweet home. Therefore, the cat was less likely to get stressed. But, what about the owner's jumper or bedding? Some of the items were not old and even appeared to be brand new. We even had one customer who provided a beautiful blue Cashmere jumper. So, what were we to do about cleaning all the jumpers, cardigans or bedding which had been soiled?

Well, we had to wash them, of course.

We had no choice!

Can you imagine finding one of those sloppy turds accompanied by cat pee, wrapped in a nice pink fluffy Angora cardigan? For sure, it was not a good idea to present a once lovely cardigan back to an owner when it was covered in crap stains. There was absolutely no way that we would have handed back any jumpers or cardigans to the unsuspecting owners in that state. What would the owners think? For sure, they would have blamed us for the dastardly deed almost as if we had crapped on it ourselves. For certain, they would spread the word about our 'dirty cattery' and we would soon be out of business.

Therefore, we had to remove any trace of our feline friend's misbehaviour. So, we just covered up the cat's crime, said nothing and washed it. On the rare occasion when a cat had soiled its bedding and it was just too disgusting to wash, we had no choice but to throw it away. Then, especially if it was a beautiful jumper, we had the disconcerting job of informing the owner that their cat had crapped on it and ruined it.

Because we needed to keep the bedding clean, especially the items that had been brought in by customers, I purchased an industrial washing machine.

Can you imagine what Kathy would have said if I had used our own?

Well, that story wasn't too bad, but here comes...

Stubby

Okay, squeamish readers...

GO AWAY, NOW!!!

I certainly recommend that you don't eat while reading this, (especially chocolate) because this is a short, disgusting story about an old black Labrador named Stubby. I have changed his name because I don't want to embarrass his lady owner if she just happens to read this gruesome story.

Stubby was getting on in years and like a lot of old Labradors, grossly overweight. Greedy Labradors can be likened to walking vacuum cleaners and our friend Stubby was a typical four-legged example. Over the years, we had got to know Stubby quite well and a more pleasant placid character would be hard to meet.

But I always kept my hands well away from his

mouth and I most certainly would not kiss him.

Even though he was a good looker for his age.

This was because Stubby had a problem…

A BIG, BIG PROBLEM!!!

No, he didn't have doggy B. O. (body odour) or bad breath, it was nothing like that.

Unfortunately, he had a disgusting habit, translated into layman's terms...

He loved to eat crap!!!

Especially, dog crap!!!

'ARGHHH!!!'

Well, I did advise you not to read this.

Well, it is not too late. You can stop now if you wish.

Now, our friend Stubby didn't just eat ordinary crap. No, he was a real dog crap connoisseur. I suppose you could compare him to gourmets who eat game. (Game is the flesh of any wild animal or bird, such as the deer family, pheasants, partridge, grouse, duck etc.) Game connoisseurs like the flesh best when it has been hung for two or even three weeks. They say that it enhances the flavour.

And, that was just how Stubby liked his turds!!!

WELL HUNG!

The turds had to be a few weeks old allowing them to develop a tasty flavour for good old Stubby to savour. Stubby was an absolute expert at finding those ripe old turds as he walked our woodland circuit. He managed to sniff them out from under all sorts of undergrowth, such as bracken, briars and nettles.

I suppose you could compare Stubby to a pig, seeking and snuffling out truffles in ancient oak woodlands.

And our woodland had a lot of oak trees!

I wonder if this made a difference to the flavour of Stubby's favourite food.

'Aged in oak' is a well-known sales recommendation for superb wine or whisky.

When we walked Stubby, we kept a wary eye

on him because his disgusting turd eating was most certainly a habit that we did not want to encourage. Not only was it a horrible sight to witness, also, it made our stomachs turn and we even wretched at times. Surely it couldn't have been particularly good for old Stubby's health either, so we did our utmost best to prevent his turd-hunting habit.

But he was a devious old chap was our Stubby.

Because he could catch you out quite often.

And he did...

His favourite ploy was when he was cocking his leg up to have a pee. He could be in full flow, and then all of a sudden, when we least expected it he would take us completely by surprise and make a powerful lunge into the briars almost pulling us off our feet. If the lunge was a success, he would reappear with a fat old grey turd hanging from either side of his mouth. The poor unfortunate turd had probably started life brown and shiny.

After three fast wide opened jawed chomps, he would throw his head back and expertly turn the turd around in his mouth making it easier for him to swallow. Then he would quickly toss his head back again and you could see the large struggling turd disappear down his pink cavernous throat.

He looked just like a crocodile swallowing its prey!

Next, he licked his lips showing us just how much he had appreciated his mouthwatering meal provided by nature.

Well, what could be more natural?

So, has your stomach turned yet?

Well, don't say that I didn't warn you!

SO, READ ON IF YOU DARE...

Perhaps I should have informed Stubby's owner about his gourmet habits, but of course, I never did. Maybe she already knew about his unique palette. But if she didn't, she might have thought that we hadn't been feeding him properly. Believe me, good old Stubby ate an enormous amount of food as well as the more than ripe delicacies that he had hunted down in the oak woods.

If I had informed Stubby's owner of his disgusting habits, I don't know who would have been more embarrassed. The lady or me?

Now, my next observations do not bear thinking about...

On far too many occasions, I have observed dog owners who have come to collect their dogs greet them by kneeling down and letting them lick their faces. And sometimes, their lips.

And even their teeth!!!

YUK!!!

And we all know that dogs enjoy licking their own and other dog's private parts...

So, let us hope that Stubby's lady owner didn't let him lick her face or even worse...

Her mouth!!!

I would like to point out that I have, never ever in my life, let any dog lick my face. Or even my hands if I could help it.

Perhaps now you know the reason why!

So, did you enjoy or endure Stubby's delicious gourmet story?

Well, the next story involves a septic tank, and we all know what they store...

If you don't know, here is the clue...

A four-letter word beginning with the letter...S.

The Septic Tank

There were rare occasions when the majority of our canine guests were very clean and did not crap in their runs. They did us the favour of waiting until they were on their walk in the woods. This was sheer luxury for us, meaning it saved us a lot of time with no dog crap to shovel up. As a bonus, the degenerating dog waste fertilised the woodland soil. When the kennels were full to the brim it was usually a third of the dogs that couldn't, or wouldn't wait.

And that was certainly a lot of dog crap!

Our staff soon got used to shovelling crap and the sooner it was shovelled up the better.

So, our very first task every morning was to shovel up s**t.

Whoops sorry, dog crap!

We shovelled up the mountains of crap by using short-handled shovels and then slid it into large yellow buckets half-filled with plain water. (One bucket and shovel per kennel block.)

Each yellow bucket was known to our staff as…

The Muck Bucket.

Now, isn't that a pleasant name?

Besides the jet washer/power hose, The Muck Bucket was one of the most used items on the premises.

I discovered that if we half-filled The Muck Bucket with water, the crap that was shovelled up dropped to the bottom and sank, therefore getting rid of the smell. To me, it was just the same idea as a toilet pan.

In fact, it was a mobile toilet pan.

And, it did not take us many minutes to fill each bucket.

So, every morning, as we entered each kennel block armed with our Muck Buckets and shovels frenzied barking erupted and the majority of dogs would be standing on their hind legs with tails swishing in a bid to be the first in the queue for their morning walk. Far too often, their tails will have obtained some crap or pee during the night. I hate to think what some of them may have got up to during those dark hours. One breed of dog that we had to be particularly wary of was the Golden Retriever because they have one of the hairiest tails in the canine tribe. And let's not forget those cumbersome paws that had the main ambition of attacking our clean clothing if we were daft enough to let them jump up. For sure, I wasn't daft enough, but our keen young staff did not seem to mind what state their clothing got into.

Goodness knows what their parents thought!

When the Muck Buckets were almost full, we tipped them into a covered manhole situated near the car park. The manhole cover was directly above the septic tank and when we emptied each bucket there was a satisfying echoing splosh.

Emptying the Muck Buckets full of crap was an art in itself and was never anyone's favourite job. Sometimes the watery crap splashed back as we emptied the stinking contents. Therefore, we had to be ultra-careful and keep well out of the way of any flying particles that did their utmost to splatter our faces. If the odd splash landed on our hands or even our arm it wasn't too bad, but a direct hit on our faces happened occasionally. Especially on windy days!

'ARGHHH!'

Well, there is one thing about it, we most certainly kept our mouths clenched shut when we did that unpleasant job!

Because we had so much of the stinking fermenting liquid, the large tank needed emptying three times a year.

I am sure you can imagine that when the tank was emptied...

THE SMELL WAS ABSOLUTELY DREADFUL!!!

I always used the same contractor to empty the tank and I made sure that he came on a Sunday afternoon when we were closed. We certainly did not want any customers around when that stinking event was taking place. Goodness knows what our customers would have thought if they had smelt that volume of dog crap being sucked into the tank of the contractor's lorry that was spread on farmers fields immediately after leaving our premises.

Although we kept the kennels scrupulously clean during the day, we had no control over the shenanigans our canine guests got up to overnight. So, by now you must realise why we bathed every dog at the end of each stay.

Rupert

Now after that wonderful insight into running a boarding kennel is digested and just to tone things down a little bit, let us move on to an amusing story about a little dog named Rupert.

And what happened with his crap...

On numerous weekends, Ann, Kathy's sister who lived with us at the time, often brought her boss's dog to board in our kennels.

Ann was the personnel manager for a small building firm which was based near Market Drayton, not too far from our pet hotel. The little dog's name was Rupert. He was a Kerry Blue Terrier which is quite a rare breed. In fact, over the years he was the only dog of that breed that ever visited our premises. Rupert was a very lively curly-coated little dog full of fun and energy and he had a very nice temperament as well.

Bear in mind, that a DENSE CURLY COAT can hide all manner of things!

Facts about Kerry Blue Terriers

Kerry Blue Terriers are born black and their coat gradually fades to grey, acquiring its adult solid slate grey/blue colour by 18 months. They are working dogs bred to hunt rodents and herd sheep. They are loyal, lovable, bold, and strong-minded dogs. They are protective and make great family pets. They are hypoallergenic, which causes fewer allergic reactions due to their coat type, and the absence of loose fur, making them suitable for people with allergies to dogs. They have a long head, flat skull, deep chest, and a soft wavy-to-curly coat that comes in several shades of grey/blue, the general term outside this breed being progressive grey. They weigh around 40 lbs (15-18 kg) and their height is 20 ins (46-51 cm).

Facts about Ann

Ann is a petite lady with a height of five feet two inches. She is a brunette with a neatly cut pageboy hairstyle. Take note, Ann's hair is the clue in Rupert's story.

In the early days before we employed numerous staff, Ann often helped to walk the dogs, feed the cats and afterwards go for a very welcoming hot shower before she nipped off to work.

So, here comes the build-up!

Ann was always very particular about her appearance and like her three sisters, quite attractive too. (I have to say that. Don't I?)

One Monday morning, Ann was taking Rupert back to work where she was to hand him over to her boss. Rupert had been for his early morning walk around our woodland circuit and had been a very good boy and done his 'business'. Ann had a red Ford Fiesta hatchback. To accommodate Rupert's large travelling cage, she was able to take out the back window shelf. This enabled

Rupert to see where he was going and Ann could keep an eye on him in her rearview mirror. During their journey for some reason only known to Rupert, he was very excitable and was non-stop bouncing about in his cage.

Eventually, Ann arrived at work and delivered the excited little Rupert back to her boss at his house which was almost as big as a mansion. Then she walked over to her nearby office which was part of a lovely converted barn.

On that particular Monday, Ann was conducting interviews. The building firm was expanding and needed one more member of staff. The first two interviews went quite well, but Ann had noticed the interviewees seemed to stare at her quite strangely. Before Ann called for the third one, she decided to go to the ladies room to check her appearance.

Ann glanced in the mirror, but could not see anything untoward with her reflection. She returned to her office sat behind her desk and called in the third hopeful interviewee. The third person, who incidentally was a man, seemed to be taking a keen interest in her. Ann thought that maybe he was more interested in her than the job! So, Ann dismissed him and called in the fourth person who was female. She also gave Ann strange looks.

The fifth person was another female. She was about twenty-five years old and her name was Jan. Ann took to Jan and the interview was progressing well, but Ann could see that she was also looking at her strangely.

Ann thought,

'Right, that's it. I've had enough of this. I'm going to ask her what she is looking at!'

"Jan I hope you don't mind me asking, but you seem to be staring at me. Is there something wrong?"

"Well, actually, there is. I hope you don't mind me telling you, but you seem to have something stuck in your hair."

To say the least, Ann was extremely embarrassed!

"Oh no! Thanks for telling me. Can you please excuse me for a moment? I'm just going to the ladies room to check."

Ann left the interview and almost ran to the ladies room for another look in the mirror. This time, she really scrutinised herself.

And that's when she spotted it...

'ARGHHH!!!'

As we all know, a brunette's hair colour is dark brown, almost black.

And as you read earlier, Ann is a brunette.

Here comes the problem...

Camouflaged halfway down Ann's hair on the right side of her face was...

Something....

A small lump of a dark brown substance clinging to her hair.

To Ann's horror, it dawned on her exactly what it was.

Dog crap!

Rupert's dog crap!

'RUPERT! RUPERT! WHAT HAVE YOU DONE?'

It was a piece of crap about the size of a

thumbnail.

'ARGHHH!!!'

'RUPERT I'LL KILL YOU!!!'

Words could not describe the extreme embarrassment Ann felt at that moment. No wonder all the interviewees had been looking at her strangely.

Perhaps the guy she interviewed didn't fancy her after all!

As fast as humanly possible, Ann cleaned the sticky stuff off her hair with tissue paper as it clung like putty. As she frantically cleaned Rupert's crap out of her hair, she most certainly was not looking forward to facing the music by going back into her office to complete the interview with Jan.

'W*hat the devil am I going to say to her?'*

As Ann entered the office, her face was burning bright red with embarrassment.

In a flurry of stuttering words, Ann cut Jan's interview short by saying,

"Well Jan, I think you are just what we are looking for. I will be in touch with you within the week."

Still extremely embarrassed, Ann hustled Jan out of the office and with a big sigh of relief closed the door turned her back on it and almost sliding down pressed herself against it.

'*Thank goodness that was the last interview!*'

Taking a few minutes to recover from her embarrassing ordeal, Ann shot back to the ladies room to methodically clean her hair. Although Ann put loads of soap on her hair, the faint pungent smell of Rupert's crap haunted her all day long.

After Ann's day of work had finished, (and it couldn't come soon enough) when she arrived at our premises, she leapt out of her car and ran into the cottage to get to the shower and was not satisfied until she had shampooed her hair several times.

The good news was, Jan the last interviewee who had been brave enough to inform Ann about Rupert's crap in her hair was employed by the building firm and they became good friends. In fact, they still keep in touch with each other to this day. But it was a long time before Ann and Jan discussed the subject of Rupert's crap that lurked in Ann's hair on that memorable Monday.

When they were better acquainted Jan said,

"I knew all along it looked like dog muck, but I just couldn't imagine how it could possibly have got there. I was hoping you were going to employ me and I certainly didn't want to upset you. I was so pleased when you asked me what I was looking at because if you hadn't, I'm not sure how I was going to pluck up the courage to tell you."

Well, we have certainly laughed many times over that story.

All I can say is, it could have been worse. It could have happened to me!

Sammy

Most dogs that came to us were more than likely very clean at home. Well, for their owner's sake, I sincerely hope so. Because I can tell you now, with some of the sights that greeted us first thing in the morning you most certainly would not want to face every sunrise at home.

Whenever we had a lot of shitty (oh, sorry folks, a bit of a slip there) dogs boarding with us, we used to run a dirty dog competition. Each member of staff would try to beat the other with incredible crap stories about the dogs that they looked after.

Yes, this is absolutely true!

We heard tales of dogs doing various things with the crap that they had produced during the night. For instance, such as finding dogs covered in their own crap because the idiots had rolled in it!

Boarding with us was a white mongrel called Sammy. But every morning we were greeted by a brown Sammy. He had managed to change the colour of his coat to the colour of crap, in fact it was crap.

It was Sammy's crap!

Yes, Sammy used to crap in his bed and then lie in it. Perhaps he didn't want to be a white dog after all. But we were determined to keep him white. So every single day of his stay he had a bath.

Maybe he changed the colour of his coat because he was obsessed with bathing.

Who knows?

Blanco

Blanco was a white Golden Retriever, hence his name. His claim to fame was, he played a game similar to hide and seek, but his game was hide the crap.

Blanco used to crap it and hide it.

We would seek it, find it and dispose of it.

On his walks, Blanco never bothered to crap in the woods, so we always knew that there would be a large glistening turd lurking somewhere in his kennel.

Blanco hid it under his bed, in his bed, in his blanket. We even found it hidden under his upturned silver water bowl.

Our stainless steel bowls fitted snugly into steel brackets which I had designed. They were a tight fit so that the dogs could not tip their water out. The bowls sitting snugly in the brackets were virtually immovable. But Blanco was unique! He was the only dog who boarded with us that could remove his bowl from the bracket, overturn it and then hide his crap underneath it.

Often, I watched quite a few crazy dogs trying to attempt to remove their water bowls.

Goodness knows why!

But always to no avail. I don't know why the dogs wanted to remove them, but I am sure it was not for the same reason that Blanco had in mind.

It was beyond me, what tricks some dirty dogs got up to. Maybe Blanco thought he was a member of the feline species and needed to bury his crap.

Well, at least he didn't lie in it like Sammy.

Cecil

Cecil was a very clever dog he could do things with crap that you would not imagine possible.

Cecil was a Miniature Poodle, he belonged to a lady who was a breeder of Poodles. He shared his kennel with two canine girlfriends. Also Miniature Poodles.

Poodle facts

Miniature Poodles are middle-sized Poodles, with

the Toy Poodle being the smallest and the Standard Poodle being the largest. Miniature Poodles are well-known for their high emotional sensitivity and intelligence. Sir Winston Churchill had two Miniature Poodles with the same name, Rufus I and Rufus II. Miniature Poodles weigh up to 15 lbs (6.8 kg) and reach up to 15 ins tall (38.1 cm).

It is important regarding Cecil's story to note the height of Miniature Poodles.

Cecil's coat was white, the other two were light brown. The three of them had that typical French Poodle cut; the pom-pom style. Cecil's girlfriends had a single pink ribbon tied on top of their heads and the three of them smelt strongly of cheap perfume. I am not an expert on perfume, but to me, the overpowering sweet sickly smell that wafted up into the depths of my nostrils was a definite turn-off.

Now, clever Cecil produced turds that ended up in a very strange place indeed.

You won't believe where we found his turds.

My Goodness! They were staring back at us as they clung onto the dividing four-foot wall of his run.

But the turds were not on the top of the wall which was impossible for him to reach. No, Cecil's turds were glued to the side of the wall. The amazing thing is, the turds were not perched near the bottom, but fairly high up. In fact, the turds were stuck halfway up the wall well over two feet from the base of the concrete floor.

How on earth had little Cecil managed to perform that engineering feat?

Perhaps he was helped by his two lady friends and he stood on their backs.

The other question was. Why on earth did he stick his turds on the wall in the first place?

Perhaps he did it at home.

Maybe in the lounge!

The Poodles owner had informed me that she kept the three posh Poodles who were show dogs inside her house. I suppose Cecil must have been getting some practice somewhere.

Perhaps, he had been a plasterer in a previous life, because he was good.

Very good indeed!

Every morning when we entered Cecil's run we found his turds perched halfway up the wall.

And beautifully formed as well!

Unfortunately for Cecil, on the odd occasion, one or two turds had slid down. Perhaps he had made a mistake with the consistency. Maybe they were too firm to stick. We knew they were his because Cecil's girlfriends did their 'business' in the woods and Cecil never did anything other than a pee. As we scraped his precious turds off the wall he used to yap like crazy. Obviously, he did not want us to remove them.

Can you imagine if Cecil had been with us for two weeks and we had not removed any of his turds?

How many would there have been?

It is 'Beggars belief' how that wall would have looked!

To say that the wall would have resembled pebble-dash would be a very good description.

Perhaps he did not like the green wall and he

preferred it brown?

It did cross my mind to ask Cecil's owner,

"What colour are the walls in your house?"

"Oh, brown of course."

Surely, that would not have been her reply!

But I bet they were not green like Cecil's run.

We concluded that the only feasible way for Cecil to get his turds so high up the wall was, he would have had to do a canine version of a handstand. A bit like our friend Percy the West Highland Terrier who belonged to the laughing policeman in the first book in this series. As Cecil performed his handstand he must have pressed his bum on the wall to get his turd to stick on. Cecil's turds must have been quite sticky as they slid from his body because with the force of gravity the adhesion needed to be as instant as super glue. Perhaps Cecil's two companions fell in love with him because of his acrobatic abilities. Who knows? It was a mystery to us that he was never dirty around his rear end. We just hoped that he wasn't licking himself clean!

Or even worse, maybe his companions did it for

him!

YUK!!!

I was more than curious how Cecil managed to perform his amazing feat. This resulted in me wasting quite a lot of my precious time hiding in the opposite run across the aisle. Alas, Cecil never performed as I watched. Perhaps, in his canine mind, he wanted to guard his sticky secret.

Canadian Visitors

This next story is about some very unusual unwanted visitors.

One summer's evening I was working in the office adjoining the kennel block. It was heaven! I could not hear a meow or a single dog bark to spoil the beautiful ambience of that warm still evening.

But that tranquil atmosphere did not last long...

It never does, does it?

It was not long before...

I heard a strange honking sound.

No, it was not a car horn.

It was the sound of a bird.

In fact, more than one bird.

It sounded like a gaggle of geese.

And sure enough, that is exactly what it was.

With mounting curiosity, I left the office and walked out onto the car park. To my amazement, I was greeted by a gaggle of five Canadian geese grazing the grass on the large lawn bordering the car park.

'Where the devil have you lot come from?'

The Canadian visitors seemed quite tame, making me think that they were used to people. Obviously, they had strayed from a farm near here. I knew that there would be little or no chance of them surviving the night if they were left outside to fend for themselves. For sure, they would never see another sunrise with 'Charlie Fox' on the prowl. I knew that if 'Charlie' found the gaggle of five, he would have had a field day. So I needed to catch them and find out who they belonged to. If you remember, I have mentioned in other stories that 'Charlie' is the nickname country folk, especially gamekeepers give to foxes.

I walked back into the office picked up the phone and rang Kathy who was preparing our evening meal.

She picked up and I said,

“You will never believe what has just turned up on our car park.”

“I’m intrigued, tell me.”

"A gaggle of geese.”

"What! Are you serious?”

“Well, if you don’t believe me. Come and have a look for yourself.”

So after that brief conversation, it wasn’t many minutes before Kathy joined me on the car park as I stood with my honking gaggle of new-found friends.

I asked Kathy to give me a hand to guide them to somewhere safe. I came up with the wonderful idea of temporarily moving them into the kennel kitchen which was next to the office. We set about the task and soon managed to manoeuvre and shoo the honking geese inside.

Well, it turned out to be not a very good idea...

NOT A VERY GOOD IDEA AT ALL!!!

With the geese locked safely away in the fox-proof kitchen I got on the phone and rang up our nearest neighbour David who owned the farm just across the fields. And yes, it was Margaret, David's wife who had lost the Canadian geese. David informed me that Margaret had reared them from day-olds and would leave immediately to collect them.

Within ten minutes David and Margaret arrived on the car park in a 4 x 4 to pick up my 'goosey' friends.

I informed them that the geese were safely stowed away in the kitchen, so we walked over to the door and I opened it to the sound of deafening honking. I peered around the door to see what all the deafening noise was about.

I had the shock of my life...

When I took in the horrible sight that greeted my eyes, I decided that they were not my 'goosey' friends anymore.

I just could not believe what I was looking at...

There was not a space big enough on the kitchen floor where I could have placed the palm of my hand without touching slimy green goose crap.

Well, at least the one advantage that goose crap has over cat and dog crap, there is not much of a smell to it. The disadvantage is, (the phrase, 'Loose as a goose' comes to mind) we were getting first-hand experience on how that phrase had come about. The goose crap was everywhere and as a colourful bonus, it was bright green as well.

Not Cecil's favourite colour as you will have learned earlier.

A farm machine called a muck spreader could not have done a better job. The goose crap was splattered up the walls and even on the ceiling. The geese must have panicked in their new surroundings. (Thanks to Geoff.) Obviously, the young geese had flapped their powerful wings at the same time that they were crapping, giving re-decorating the kitchen a whole new meaning.

The four of us were speechless.

So, who was going to clean up this mess?

I knew that it wasn't going to be the owners of the geese, that's for sure!

No, it would be the silly fool, meaning yours truly, who had the brilliant idea of shutting them in the kitchen in the first instance!

'ARGHHH!!!'

Jamie

So, still on the subject of crap. This short story is quite an unusual one, perhaps it would be more appropriate for me to say,

"An unusual piece of crap."

For sure, I have never seen one like it before, or since...

Can you believe?

It was blue!

We had a short-haired pointer boarding with us called Jamie. He was with us for three weeks and was yet another one of those dirty dogs that would not wait or could not wait for his walk in the woods. So the first thing every morning out would come the old faithful Muck Bucket and shovel. At least the good news was Jamie's turds always consisted of the good old rock-hard variety.

Early in the morning the day Jamie was going home, Pat called me to his run.

She said,

"Hey Geoff, come and have a look at this. You're not going to believe it!"

'Here we go again! Believe what?'

I peered into Jamie's run and there on the concrete floor lay a piece of crap.

I could only describe it as being multi-coloured. The colours consisted of various shades of brown, But its predominant colour can you believe?

Was a lovely shade of blue.

Have you ever seen a blue turd before?

Well, I certainly haven't!

More than curious, I asked,

"My Goodness, Pat. What the devil is that?"

She replied,

"It looks like rubber, or maybe plastic to me."

I decided that I would dissect the handsome turd to satisfy my curiosity. Dissect it, I bet you are thinking, UGH! How could you? Well, I can assure you, I don't like getting my fingers in the crap, just like anyone else. And getting that stuff under my fingernails does not bear thinking about. Mind you, it sure would be a great cure for stopping people from biting their nails. Luckily I have never had that problem, but I do keep my nails very short.

The plan was definitely not to use my hands, but to dissect the colourful turd with water. I rigged the power hose up, pulled the trigger and with a powerful jet of water cornered the handsome blue turd against the wall of the run.

It only took seconds before the brown was separated from the blue.

I was amazed, you will never guess what I was staring at...

Incredibly...

A rubber glove!

If we could have found the other one we would have had a nice useable pair.

Maybe the other one was yet to emerge.

Well, there was one thing for certain. The blue rubber glove was not one of ours.

The gloves we used were yellow!

Marigold's, to be precise.

So you don't have to be Einstein to work out that Jamie must have swallowed his rubber meal more than three weeks before he arrived on our premises.

Well, he certainly did not appear any worse for

wear!

Later that day, Jamie's owners came to collect him. I informed them just what Jamie had given birth to that morning.

I held up Jamie's baby.

Whoops sorry!

I mean Jamie's blue rubber glove for all to see.

Not in my bare hand of course, but with my fingers hygienically enclosed in one of our yellow Marigolds. I must say the blue glove was much cleaner than when it had left Jamie earlier that morning.

I said to Jamie's owner, Mrs Reynolds,

"Do you by any chance recognise this rubber glove?"

"I don't believe it. I lost one the same colour a few days before Jamie came here."

"Well, we found it in Jamie's run this morning!"

"Goodness gracious! That is almost four weeks ago."

I have heard of Sharks swallowing strange objects and I have heard of dogs swallowing balls and stones.

But a whole rubber glove?

That has to be a first!

Over the years, Jamie swallowing a rubber glove was not such an unusual event because we found all sorts of objects in that sticky brown stuff. But we never found any money!

Many of the owners would come in and say,

"I think '*Rover*' may have swallowed an 'item', yesterday or today."

Now that 'item' could have been a dishcloth, a sponge, a ball, a child's toy, paper, or many other manner of things. (But still no money!) The list could have gone on forever. Most of the owners never had any idea that their dog had swallowed anything at all. On many occasions, when we had strange-looking turds to dispose of we couldn't make out what the object was or had been.

All we knew was, it did not start life out as dog food!

Diarrhoea

Are you still here...

Because...

I HAVE SAVED THE BEST OR SHOULD I SAY, THE WORST UNTIL LAST!!!

This is the final story about crap and surely by now, you must be thinking...

'Thank goodness for that!'

This is the most horrible story by far and is definitely and I must emphasise definitely...

NOT FOR QUEASY STOMACHS.

So, this is my final warning. If you are

determined or brave enough to read on...

DO SO AT YOUR OWN RISK!

It was not unusual for owners to provide us with food for their cats or dogs. In fact, we encouraged it. It was not feasible for us to stock every brand of tinned cat and dog food, so we just stocked the most popular.

In the latter years, we were so well established that the amount of tinned food ordered amounted to several pallets delivered by large trucks on a regular basis. Often, it took an hour or so to unload and then restack the variation of tins and bags of food in our storeroom. Of course, all this food was processed into crap by our animal friends and obviously, the total number of Muck Buckets rose too.

In our paperwork system, (before we were computerised) every cat or dog booking form doubled as a questionnaire. One of the most important questions was, what brand of food do you feed your cat or dog? So, if we didn't have it in stock, we advised the owners to supply their own and then we gave them a reduction on their bill. For sure, it is not advisable to change a cat or dog's diet, especially when it is going to be eating and sleeping in a strange environment. Change is not good, so we did our best to keep the animals boarding with us on the same food. The food agreed with them at home, so it should agree with them when they boarded with us.

My motto is...

NEVER CHANGE A PET'S DIET, UNLESS IT IS ABSOLUTELY NECESSARY!

Not only could a change of diet cause stress, but more often than not, it created the very worst form of crap known as…

Diarrhoea.

Therefore, diarrhoea caused stress amongst the staff, especially when first thing in the morning they had to clear the stinking mess up.

Not the nicest of jobs to tackle after enjoying a full English breakfast. Especially if the eggs were really runny!

I suppose it might have been worse, we could have been shovelling diarrhoea before eating breakfast.

THIS IS WHERE THE STORY GETS WORSE.

MUCH! MUCH! WORSE!!!

ARE YOU REALLY SURE THAT YOU WANT TO READ ON?

Okay, so you're still with me. Here it comes, the story that you have been waiting for...

One sunny Saturday afternoon, three dogs arrived, they were lovely Border Collies. Shep, Jed and Suzy. Their lady owner proudly informed me that Shep, Jed and Suzy had won numerous trophies in agility competitions.

She provided their food which was fresh raw minced meat contained in polythene bags. One bag for each day of their stay. Shep, Jed and Suzy were going to be with us for seven days. So we put six bags in our large chest freezer and kept one bag out for their evening meal.

As the Border Collie's proud owner left the office she hit me...

With this parting statement,

"As a treat, because I feel sorry for leaving them, I started them on minced meat this morning."

'Not a good idea to change their food. Today, of all days!'

But with her being a show person, surely she should know what she was doing. I mean, if she didn't know what her dogs should be eating...

Then who would?

Who was I to disagree?

I never thought any more of it as I took Shep, Jed and Suzie on their introductory walk. As we walked around the woodland circuit, I couldn't help but notice how nice and glossy their coats were. Obviously, they were in tip-top condition.

And I most certainly intended to keep them that way.

When our young staff walked dogs around our woodland circuit, in their training they had been instructed by me or my manager to watch every dog perform their 'business'.

Yes, check their crap!

If there were likely to be any health problems, it usually showed up in their crap first. This could often give us a forewarning of any illness. As I walked around the circuit, I watched all three Border Collies do their 'business' and each did a perfectly formed stool. I noted all three stools matched each other in colour and hardness. I had become quite an expert on the subject of crap and I could see we were going to have no problem at all with these three lively characters. Yes, they were full of life, absolutely typical of the Border Collie breed just full of boundless energy.

Little did I know that wasn't going to last for long...

NOT LONG AT ALL!!!

Early the following morning, I was walking across the lawned area from the cottage towards the block of kennels as I whistled away without a care in the world. It was a beautiful spring day and a blackbird was whistling away.

I was about sixty yards away from the kennel buildings when I looked up to see my manager Kick. (A nickname she retained from her school days.) She was coming out of the first block of kennels next to the office.

She spotted me and beckoned furiously as she yelled,

"GEOFF! GEOFF! COME HERE QUICK!"

'Oh No! Here we go again! My tranquil world is going to burst like a balloon. I know it.'

I broke into a run and sprinted the distance between us. Did all this sprinting keep me fit or what?

The expression on her ghostly white face was one of severe shock.

Kick could barely utter the words,

"I was just about to phone you."

"What's up now?" You look as if you've seen a ghost."

"You had better come in here quick and look at this!"

I hurried after her into the kennel block and as I did...

A VILE SMELL HIT ME LIKE A SLEDGEHAMMER!!!

It was a smell that will stay with me for the rest of my days. It was a very strong meaty aroma invading my nostrils and throat!

'What is that?'

The more than awful smell reminded me of the horrible aroma emitted from butchers shops years ago. I vividly remember the sawdust scattered all over the floor. Presumably, the sawdust was there to soak up any blood! But that retching smell in our kennel block was ten times stronger than any butchers shop causing my stomach to heave with rising bile.

For sure, I knew that whatever the smell was, it had to relate to some kind of terrible...

MAJOR CATASTROPHE!!!

Kick, now even whiter in the face if that is possible, led me down the centre aisle where we finally arrived outside the run belonging to Shep, Jed and Suzy.

The sight that greeted my eyes was unbelievable!

'Oh no! Of all the dogs in these kennels it would have to be these.'

I would never have thought that three dogs could produce so much diarrhoea!

THERE LOOKED TO BE GALLONS AND GALLONS OF THE GREEN STINKING STUFF!

The three Collies were shivering and standing motionless right in the middle of it. The poor dogs had no choice because the concrete floor was absolutely covered in it. The glutinous diarrhoea was everywhere. It was even splattered underneath the roof of their run. They were unrecognisable. Their once gleaming black and white coats were matted from head to toe in dreadful green stinking diarrhoea. I reached into the pocket of my jeans and pulled out a large white handkerchief to cover my nose and mouth. The smell of diarrhoea was so intense that it made me go weak at the knees and I had an overwhelming feeling of wanting to puke.

Kick, with all her canine experience sobbed,

"Geoff, I am really sorry, but I just can't stomach this. I cannot clean this kennel out!"

'Nor can I!'

With the vile task that confronted us, I didn't blame her one little bit.

Well, someone had to clean the awful mess up.

Awful mess, is a gross understatement.

As usual, here we go again...

The buck stops with me!

But, how on earth was I going to cope?

Just looking at the slimy stinking diarrhoea was stomach-retching enough...

And I knew once it was disturbed...

The vile smell would get even...

Worse!!!

NO DOUBT ABOUT IT!!!

That aroma of raw minced meat that had passed rapidly through those poor dogs was the worst smell I had ever had to cope with in my life. In fact, the smell was so strong you could almost see it in the air.

I was sure that this was going to be the worst job I had to tackle in my life.

Thank goodness!

All of a sudden…

I had an idea…

I hurried down to our garage where I kept my tools and returned with an industrial rubber mask. I used the mask to protect myself from the spray when I used my backpack sprayer for killing weeds. It was a great idea because I knew nothing and I mean nothing, not even gas could penetrate that mask.

Especially, the smell of…

Diarrhoea!

Dressed in a blue boiler suit, rubber gloves, (yellow Marigolds, not Jamie's blue one!) topped off with the rubber mask. I entered the Border Collie's run.

I must have looked like I was about to tackle some sort of nuclear catastrophe!

Well, it was close!

My first task was to evacuate the severely

subdued Border Collies. Taking the utmost care, I cajoled them into the adjoining run. Then using a hosepipe, I gently hosed them down to get the worst of the sticky stinking goo off.

Luckily the shitty (I am not apologising) liquid was diluted by the water.

In turn, I led each Collie out of their temporary run into our grooming room to be shampooed. Two of our staff, sisters Tracey and Haley had volunteered for the horrible task.

Once the Collies had been vacated from their second run, I set up the power hose. Normally, it would take me three minutes to jetwash and disinfect a kennel and run.

But in this instance…

It took me well over an hour!!!

The first thing Kick did was phone the vet. He requested that we clean the dogs before he arrived.

He was no fool!

And who could blame him?

Within minutes of him arriving on our premises, he diagnosed that the three Border Collies had got severe gastroenteritis brought on by eating food which was far too rich.

I could have told him that!

Following the vet's strict instructions, we treated the sorrowful Collies with the medication that he had prescribed.

The good news was…

Shep, Jed and Suzy were as right as rain within three days.

Of course, we had more diarrhoea to clear up during that day, but fortunately nowhere near the amount that had been produced the previous night.

A week later, when their owner arrived to pick them up, I had no choice.

I had to!

And I wanted to!

Inform her what had happened to her lovely

Border Collies.

After a mild rollicking from me, she said that with her vast experience, she really should have known better.

'You're not kidding!'

The good news is, after their horrible ordeal, (and ours) she boarded Shep, Jed and Suzie with us on numerous occasions. And thankfully, never tried to bring mincemeat again. For sure, if she had I would have refused it.

Anyway, to CRAP it all, (I do mean CAP it all) this is one crap story, I did not want to talk about at dinner that night...

Or in fact, any night ever!!!

Well, I do hope that you were not too shocked by my crap stories, but I can assure you they are absolutely true.

I have used the word crap almost one hundred times and because I used the word...

S. H. I. T.

To occasionally elaborate, I sincerely apologise.

Anyway, I hope the word crap, made it a little bit more pleasant to read.

SO, WHO WANTS TO RUN A PET HOTEL NOW???

CHAPTER 18

Twelve Harleys and...A Hearse!

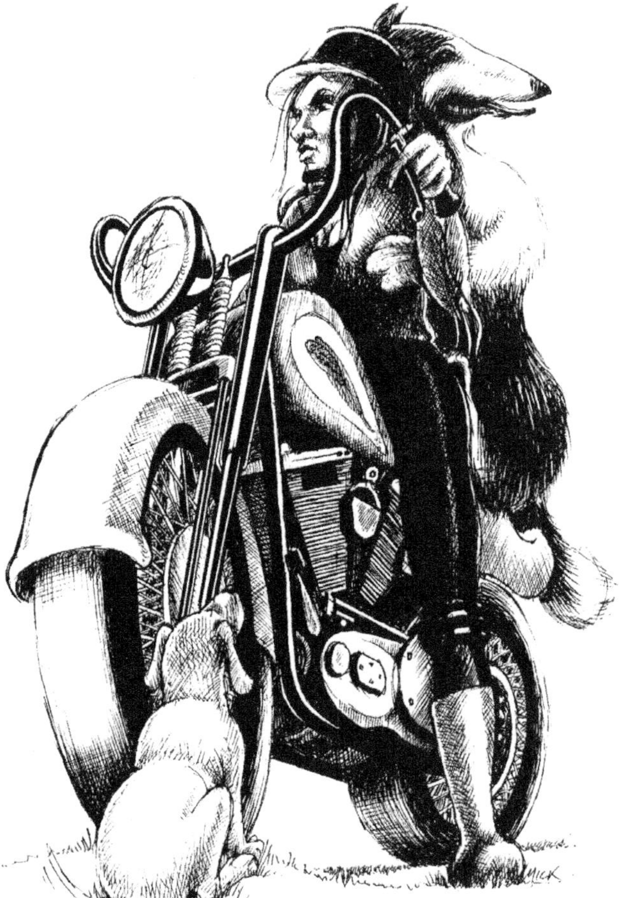
MICK

Okay, after all that crap, let's get back to some form of normality.

Lassie

This story gave me a jaw-dropping surprise. It revolves around Lassie a Rough Collie.

Rough Collie facts

The Rough Collie originates from the Scottish Highlands where they were used for herding cattle and sheep. In the 1860s, Queen Victoria discovered the Rough Collie when visiting Balmoral Castle in Scotland. The royal seal of approval immediately caused demand for the breed to boom. By 1877, Collies were being shown at the Westminster Kennel Club show where wealthy dog lovers, including J.P. Morgan, took them up. From 1954 to 1973, the Rough Collie saw a massive worldwide increase in popularity, thanks to the T.V. show Lassie which aired at that time. Actually, Lassie was portrayed as female, but over the years when the series ran, her part was played by eleven males. Modern Rough Collies are not generally used for traditional herding duties. However, they are popular as assistance dogs aiding people with disabilities. These active dogs also enjoy a new career as family pets.

One morning I was walking up to the kennels from our cottage when I spotted a shiny motorbike mirrored by the sun. It was parked on the car park outside the office and it looked like the owner had left a bag hanging from the handlebars. I have never been into motorbikes, although I admire the look of them. I am sure that if I had owned one when I was young, I probably would have been long-dead by now. In my youth, I was crazy enough in a car, so I dread to think what I would have been like on a motorbike. I couldn't help but admire the glistening motorbike. To satisfy my curiosity, I walked up to it and read the make on the metallic crimson-coloured fuel tank. It was a Harley-Davidson.

After admiring the fabulous-looking machine, I walked into the office where Pat and a lady customer were sitting on either side of the office desk chatting away like long-lost friends. Pat introduced me to the lady who was wearing a tight black leather suit. So, it didn't take me too many seconds to deduce that she was the rider of the glistening Harley.

I got into a conversation with the leather-clad lady and it transpired that she was not the owner of the Harley. She had borrowed it from her boyfriend.

Little did I know that I was going to meet up with him later.

The leather-clad lady whose name was Jane booked in Lassie her Rough Collie.

With Lassie booked in, Jane fired up the Harley and with a thunderous roar disappeared down the drive on the wondrous machine.

As I listened to the throbbing engine fading away, I thought that I would be more than interested to see how Lassie was going to be transported to our premises on the back of a Harley-Davidson.

A few weeks later, I had forgotten all about Lassie's booking and on the day that she arrived, I was outside the cattery building when I heard the throb of powerful engines. Puzzled, I looked in the direction of the sound that was getting louder by the second and to say that I was astonished would be an understatement.

It was a pack of Hells Angels!!!

'What?'

Knowing the violent reputation that Hells Angels have in movies, a thought flashed through my mind,

'Shall I fetch my double-barreled shotgun?'

Bravely and gunless, I marched up to the car park. As it turned out, I had nothing to worry about from the fearful-looking bearded riders because they were only escorting a dog.

It was Jane's Lassie.

I must say that I was a little bit disappointed because Jane's lovely Lassie arrived in the back of a Renault Cleo.

Not on the back of a Harley Davidson!

The Renault Cleo driven by Jane, was escorted by twelve of the nicest bikers it would have been anyone's pleasure to meet. All on Harleys.

In a previous phone conversation, unknown to me, Pat and Jane had organised the Renault Cleo to stay on our car park for the duration of Lassie's stay. The car would remain parked there as Jane and the pack of magnificent machines toured the scenic country of Wales. I knew nothing of these arrangements and that was why a pack of Hells Angels arriving on our car park had been a complete surprise to me.

As Pat and Jane chatted in the office, probably about Lassie's booking. The twelve Harleys were parked in a glistening line running from the office all the way along the car park. The gang of Hells Angels stood in a group nearby laughing and joking. I just couldn't resist walking over to admire the impressive machines where I struck up an interesting conversation with the gang of bikers who were sporting skull and cross-bone emblems on their black leathers. One of the bearded bikers was Jane's boyfriend who turned out to be a very nice guy. Jane in matching leathers was the only female amongst the gang.

After Jane had said goodbye to Lassie, she climbed onto the back of her boyfriend's Harley and as she swung her leg over the back pillion, she gave Pat and me a wink and a cheery wave.

The pack of throbbing bikes roared away in unison all the way down our long drive, then turning right onto the A41 highway we could hear the 'Angels' opening up their throttles with a roar as they started their exciting journey towards Wales.

Standing with Pat and Lassie, I turned and said,

"Well, we have had a dog arrive in a Police car." (Percy in book one.)

"Now we have Hells Angels riding onto our car park."

"Whatever is next?"

WELL, HERE IT COMES!

Jake

It was a sunny Friday morning in July and I was sitting at my desk in the cottage study writing bookings into the cat and dog diaries. Suddenly, I was startled by a loud rapping sound on the window that made me almost jump out of my skin. I looked up through the window and there was Kathy.

She beckoned and shouted,

"GEOFF, GEOFF, COME QUICK!"

"Here we go again! What has happened now?

I leapt to my feet and shot out through the front door where Kathy was waiting on the path by the garden gate.

Puzzled, I said,

"What's up?"

Kathy pointed and said,

"Look over to the car park!"

Curious, I stared at the car park over a hundred yards away.

I could not believe what I was looking at.

Was I having a black comedy dream?

Because...

Parked on the car park by the office was...

Can you believe it?

A HEARSE!!!

Now, those vehicles have always given me the creeps and still do. And now we have one on our car park!

I gave an involuntary shiver, looked at Kathy and said,

"What the devil is going on?"

"I don't know. Your guess is as good as mine. I just spotted it and then I came to tell you."

So, to satisfy our curiosity we decided to be brave and started to walk up to the office.

As we got nearer and I must add with grave trepidation.

Grave is the operative word here!

We stared white-faced at the hearse as we anticipated the inevitable coffin inside.

To our relief, thank Goodness there was no coffin!

But, sitting in the driving seat, was a driver dressed in the usual black regalia of mourning, reading a newspaper.

But where the coffin normally would have been...

Sat a black dog!

'A dog???'

As we neared the office, we could hear Pat's

familiar laughter coming from within.

Puzzled and more curious than ever, Kathy and I entered the office only to discover one of our regular customers, Mrs Lowe, sitting at the office desk talking to Pat. Even more puzzling, Mrs Lowe was dressed from head to toe in black.

'What is going on here?'

Still puzzled, I said,

"Hello Mrs Lowe, what are you up to today?"

Without answering my question, she said,

"Hello there, Mr and Mrs Doody. Pat and I didn't think it would be too long before you turned up. We thought that when you saw the hearse you might think that you had a dead body on your premises."

With that, Mrs Lowe and Pat burst into hearty laughter. Getting the joke, Kathy and I joined in. We were laughing so much we had tears in our eyes.

Especially when I said,

"Any customers arriving on the car park will

think that we arrange funerals for VIP dogs now!"

Mrs Lowe had been using our kennels for several years and during all that time I never cottoned on to the fact that she ran one of the largest undertaking businesses in Stoke-on-Trent twenty-five miles away.

The reason we had a hearse on the car park was because Mrs Lowe was going on holiday the next day. She had decided to drop off her black Labrador Jake on the way to pick up (to my horror) a dead body from our local area and take it back to Stoke-on-Trent.

I said to the three laughing ladies,

"I can't imagine an undertaker having a dog any other colour than jet black."

And that set us off again...

Mrs Lowe laughed and said,

"Well, that's killed two birds with one stone!"

This resulted in the jovial lady in black leaving the premises to continue her morbid journey with our laughter ringing in her ears.

CHAPTER 19

Three very different stories about staff

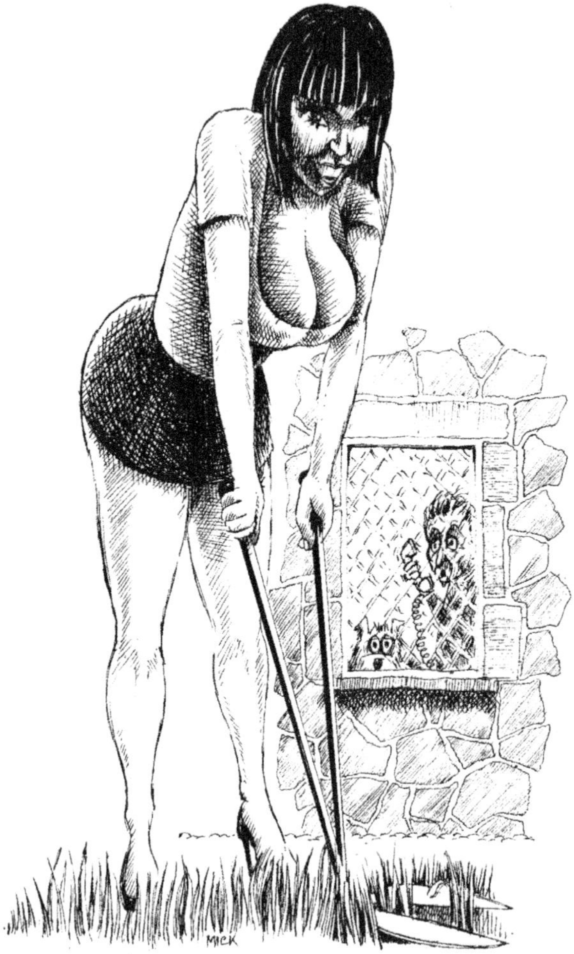
MICK

Amusing stories revolving around some of our staff.

When you are looking after animals, whether it is on a farm, a zoo, or a boarding establishment like ours, the work cannot be neglected. Come rain or shine, man's best friends have to be fed and watered and their housing kept spotlessly clean. If one of our staff did not turn up, another member had to do their work. And one member of staff missing from a small team leaves a gaping hole in that workforce.

In the latter years when we were incredibly busy, the person who filled that gap would very often be one of our managers, often making it impossible for that person to have a full lunch hour or finish work on time. And of course, I would always offer my help to do whatever was necessary.

Over the years we had four managers who were very conscientious, loyal and hard-working. They were always pleasant to our customers and very good at dealing with all the staff we employed, whatever situation occurred.

Unfortunately, on rare occasions, we had staff who let us down, not caring who was going to fill in for them. Yes, of course, there were genuine illnesses, but I often felt sometimes that was not always the case. Throughout our years in the animal boarding business, we were lucky and had a backbone of conscientious, loyal, hard-working staff to support the managers. Some of the girls (we rarely employed boys) started working part-time with us when they were as young as twelve. The reason we generally employed girls or ladies was we found them more reliable than males. (Sorry guys!)

I will never forget the day that a young girl named Jenny unexpectedly turned up on our premises with her mother to ask for a job. Jenny was a slightly built twelve-year-old. I tried to dissuade her in the nicest possible way that the work would be too much for her and that she would have to come back the following year when she would have grown taller and much stronger. I could see that she was not even tall enough to reach the top of the cat's sleeping quarters. When it came to dogs, I was worried that big strong dogs would pull her over. But Jenny was a very determined young lady who was an accomplished gymnast at school and was having none of it. She pleaded with me to give her a chance, saying that she was strong and if she could not reach anything, she would stand on something to enable her to do so. She was just so enthusiastic, and with her mother strongly backing her up. How could I refuse?

Initially, we decided that Jenny would work one day at the weekend as a trial. I was so pleased that I had given her the chance because her work was exemplary. To cut a long story short, Jenny worked with the cats and dogs every weekend including her school holidays right up to the age of eighteen.

Now this next lady, who shall remain nameless, was totally different to Jenny.

This young lady who we employed full-time was seventeen years old. On her first day, which turned out to be her last day, she turned up on her scooter smack on time. She completed the morning's work and appeared to enjoy it. When it came to her lunch hour, she asked our manager Pat if she could go home to eat her lunch because she lived only five minutes away. (Little did we know that this was a ploy.) Pat had no objection to her request even though we preferred our staff to remain on the premises. Staff remaining on the premises meant there would never be any problem with them returning late and of course, they would be there on hand if any problems arose with any of the animals.

So, off she went down our drive...

Never to be seen again!

I don't mean she disappeared off the face of the earth. She just never came back. It was a mystery because she had worked really well in the few hours that she had spent working with the animals and she had got on fine with the staff.

So, what on earth was the problem?

The next morning the mystery was solved...

Her boyfriend turned up and explained to Pat and me that his girlfriend had enjoyed the work, but had not felt at all well and would not be coming back in the very near future.

Concerned, Pat said,

"Oh dear! What is wrong with her?"

He replied,

"She felt a bit sick."

"Oh, what caused that then? Was it something she ate?"

"Oh no, nothing like that. It's probably because she's three months pregnant. I've only come to collect the money you owe her."

Now, wait for this next bit of amazing information...

"Also, I need to sort out her maternity pay."

Pat and I just looked at each other in sheer disbelief.

We were gobsmacked!!!

When I eventually got my brain back into gear again, I had a very brief conversation with the young man. It most certainly was a brief conversation because I told him in no uncertain terms to go away and not bother us again.

Actually, I could have used just two words, but I will leave that to your imagination!

Fortunately, the cheeky young man decided to vacate our premises rapidly because he could see that he was going to get nothing from me that day.

Except maybe...

My boot up his backside!

The very next thing I did was phone my solicitor, Mike, just to make sure that the pregnant young lady did not have any claim on me. (I made Mike famous in the hilarious story about Pepper in the previous book.) After I explained the full story, Mike roared with laughter.

Then he had the audacity to ask me,

"Is her pregnancy anything to do with you, Geoff?"

We both laughed at his joke.

Then he went into serious legal mode and said,

“Geoff, you have nothing to worry about, providing you pay for the work that she did yesterday morning. In fact, I recommend that you pay her for the full day.”

I paid the amount due and fortunately, that was the end of that little saga. The young pregnant lady who had completed a grand total of four hours work was never heard from again.

Neither was her conniving boyfriend!

Here comes the next young lady...

All the staff that wanted to work with our cats and dogs were usually interviewed by me and I must say the majority turned out to be excellent and stayed with us for many years.

But you always get the exception...

And I have to say, I did make the odd mistake now and again with some of my choices.

Over the phone, I arranged an interview with a young lady who was nineteen years old. Her name was Trudy and she wanted a full-time job. During our brief telephone conversation, she sounded very keen and intelligent. I was very impressed by the way that she answered the questions that I put forward. She appeared to have a very sensible attitude and was quite knowledgeable towards the needs of cats and dogs.

I had arranged with her to come out of hours because we were very busy at that time and I preferred to interview keen applicants undisturbed in the office. I informed her that we have a five-bar gate on our drive that would be closed with a sign that read in blood-red print...

CLOSED
HOURS 8 AM TO 5 PM
DANGER GUARD DOGS LOOSE

I explained to her that it would be quite safe for her to open the gate that had the alarming warning sign because we didn't own a guard dog. Only my Springer Spaniel Sally who would lick people to death. The idea of the sign was to deter customers from arriving out of hours.

I am sure you will remember the chapter MY SIGNS, which was a hilarious story in the previous book.

I was sitting in the office flicking through the pages of our diaries and checking the cat and dog bookings when a car rolled onto the car park. It was Trudy and she was absolutely spot on time. Well, there was the first point gained towards her future employment. At least the girl was punctual!

I watched her get out of the car and will never forget what she was wearing. Or should I say, almost wearing. She had a plunging neckline and possibly the shortest mini skirt on the planet.

'Am I dreaming? Is this a joke? Has one of my mates

set me up? Is this girl really applying for a job looking after cats and dogs?'

As I sat in the office with the door wide open, the unusually dressed kennel maid applicant walked across the car park towards me and I am sure that I must have been gawping as her stiletto heels made a clicking sound on the tarmac. My goodness! Her heels were so high... they made stilts look low!

'Surely my mates have set me up!'

She swayed as she took each step, just as if she was a model walking down the catwalk.

'Now I know my mates have set me up!'

'Or, have they?'

'Do you realise young lady, that our normal attire here, is Wellington boots!'

Trying to hide my astonishment, I said,

"Hello you must be Trudy, pleased to meet you."

In a pleasant voice, she replied,

"Hello, Mr Doody pleased to meet you too. Thank

you for agreeing to see me."

The young lady's appearance looked heavily influenced by Greek parentage. In fact, she was so pretty that she could have got away with being a Greek Goddess. Her glossy jet-black hair was piled up on the top of her head and she gave me a shy smile as she shook my hand in greeting.

During our conversation, I could not fault her answers to my questions and I realised that I was not involved in a joke concocted by my gamekeeping mates.

If it was a joke, it was a very good one!

Well, did she get the job?

Or not?

Well, of course, she got the job!

Ah, ah!

But what are you thinking?

No, she didn't just get the job because of her beauty. She got the job because she answered every single question that I fired at her. So, what could I do? I had no choice but to accept her. Well, you have to be fair in this world, don't you? All I had to do next was convince Kathy and the other staff, exactly why I had given the Greek Goddess the job.

Perhaps that was going to be the hardest part!

The first couple of days the Greek Goddess got along well with our staff and her work could not be faulted. If we were a little bit quiet in the middle of the day and the work with the cats and dogs had been completed, it was quite normal for the staff to do different tasks around the grounds or even gardening.

So, on her third day, the Greek Goddess was working with one of the other girls in our garden.

I was sitting in our study with the door to the dining room wide open giving me a view of our garden through the patio window. I was in mid-telephone conversation with a customer when my speech came to an abrupt stop. I couldn't help but notice the Greek Goddess who was wearing an extremely low-cut top. She was trimming the edges of our lawn with a pair of long-handled edging shears. Slowly she went past the patio window and was leaning forward as she glided by.

A baffled female voice asked on the other end of the telephone line,

"Are you still there Mr Doody?"

I stuttered,

"Oh, I'm sorry. I've just spotted quite a rare bird in my garden and it took away my concentration!"

Well, it wasn't a lie, was it?

It has to be said that the vision that I had just witnessed would have stopped most people in their tracks who worked in a similar environment to me. Because I was more used to seeing people in Barbour jackets and tweeds!

After the vision I had witnessed, I decided to have a word with Pat to ask Trudy to tone down her clothing a little bit.

Well, actually more than a bit!

The Greek Goddess's working days were Thursday to Monday, which included the weekend, our busiest days. When we got to the Sunday in her third week, she did not turn up. I must say in her defence that it was most unusual because she had been perfectly punctual in the short time that she had been with us and her work had been excellent.

Well, I have to defend her.

Don't I?

After all, it was my decision to employ her!

One of our other girls who came from the same nearby village, Hinstock, informed me that during the weekends, the Greek Goddess worked nights and was some sort of a dancer in a nightclub and maybe it was very late when she had finished work. Perhaps she could have had trouble getting up for work.

But, why had she taken our job knowing that she worked late at weekends?

Well, we never saw the Greek Goddess again.

And, we always wondered...

What kind of a dancer was she?

CHAPTER 20

Them Bones Them Bones

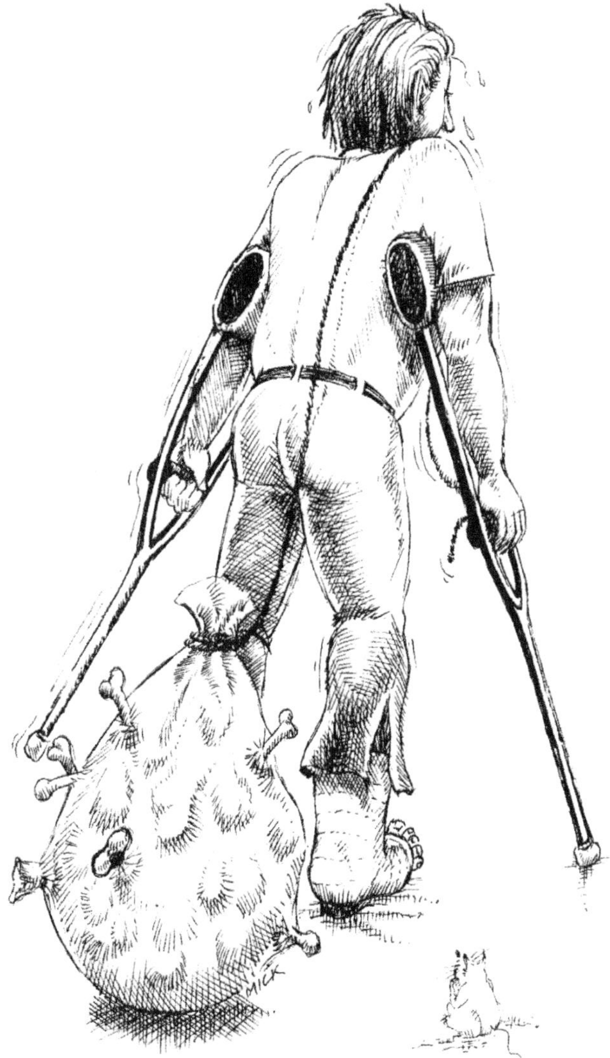
MICK

An amusing story about bones.

MY BONES!!!

Bunions to be precise!

Bunions? Bunions?

I bet you are thinking, what has bunions got to do with running a pet hotel for cats and dogs?

In my youth, I had developed very bad bunions. In fact, a massive one on each foot and eventually, they became extremely painful as well as unsightly.

Bunions are a very common complaint and over the years I have had many a conversation with friends and even strangers about each other's bunions and it often resulted in both parties taking off their shoes and socks to compare whose was the biggest and ugliest.

You could say it was a case of...

'You show me yours and I'll show you mine!'

And it was my monsters that usually got first and second prize!

People had a real shock when I took my shoes off, especially when they saw what enormous things I had managed to grow on the outside of each foot.

If they thought my left one was big, they were even more amazed when I showed them the right one.

Unfortunately, bunions can be hereditary. Not only did my parents suffer from them but also my younger sister Gail. Poor Gail had them on both feet as well. But nowhere near as big as mine!

My feet were terribly deformed and over the years I had many humorous comments made about them. One comment that comes to mind is,

"You could perch on trees with feet like those."

I was informed by my doctor that bunions should be left well alone until they start to cause real problems. And mine eventually did! I coped with the increasing pain in my feet for years until I finally had enough and made the decision to have them sorted.

The surgeon informed me that it could take up to three months for a foot to heal after a bunion has been removed. The standard medical practice was to operate on one foot at a time, ensuring that you would have the mobility to get about on the other foot. However, I insisted that I wanted both bunions removed on the same day. Also, I wanted to get it over and done with as soon as possible. I thought that if only one bunion was removed and it turned out to be excruciatingly painful then I might chicken out with the second operation. At this time, Kathy was working full-time in the business, and with plenty of staff around it was possible for me to be out of action for a while.

Before the operation, my feet really did look like I could have perched on trees with their claw-like appearance. I knew exactly what was going to take place because the surgeon had given Kathy and me a thorough briefing on everything that he intended to do.

I certainly do not like hospitals one little bit. Let's face it, who does?

So, looking much braver than I felt, I went in for the double operation…

My bunion operation took over three hours to perform and in that period the surgeon broke both big toes and cut away the two large extruding bones. In other words, the bunions from both feet. On my left foot my second toe was hammer-shaped, so he broke that and straightened it.

At last, here comes the crux of this story…

A few hours after my operation, Kathy came to visit me. I was semiconscious and deliriously talking my head off to the attending nurse.

Apparently, I asked the nurse in a very slurred voice,

"Where are my bones?"

"Don't worry Geoff, they've gone."

"But where have they gone?"

"I'm sure by now, that they are most probably in the incinerator."

I wailed,

“OH.NO!”

“What’s wrong?”

“I wanted them for the dogs.”

“What dogs?”

“The dogs at home.”

“What do you mean? You weren’t going to feed them to your dogs, were you?”

“NO! Not my dogs. The dogs in the kennels."

After that unbelievable answer, I mumbled incoherently and drifted off to sleep…

As I slept, Kathy was laughing as she explained to the amused nurse that we ran a pet hotel for cats and dogs.

On hearing that information, the nurse said,

“Whereabouts?”

Kathy answered,

"Along the A41 just north of Newport."

The nurse was flabbergasted and said,

"I don't believe it. My daughter Caroline works for you. She lives and breathes her time there and can't get enough of it."

How about that for a coincidence?

Then the nurse started talking about me and said,

"Your husband is really funny. That is the first time a patient has asked to take their bones home to feed their dogs! Wait until I tell Caroline and my colleagues about this one. Oh, and tell your husband, when he's in a fit state. If you do get short of food at the kennels, I'm sure we could save you plenty of bones before they go to the incinerator!"

Kathy hoped she was joking!

Wouldn't it have been something if I had said to a dog owner,

"Do you realise that your dog has eaten part of my feet and really enjoyed them?"

Can you imagine the look on his or her face?

The next day I was discharged from the hospital minus two massive bunions and weighing a lot lighter with all that weight taken off my feet.

So, I am sorry dogs, the incinerator got my bones first!

After five weeks, I made a full recovery and after the plaster was removed, I stared at my feet in amazement because I thought they belonged to someone else!

CHAPTER 21

A Christmas Present That Nobody Would Want!

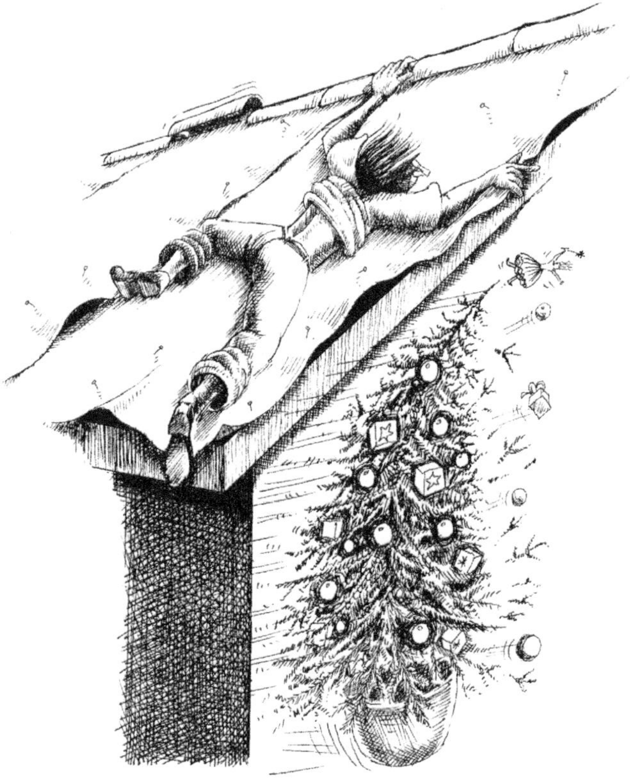

You could say, this was a rough Christmas...

Many years ago, children received Christmas

presents only if they were lucky enough to have parents who could afford them. In those far off days or to be precise, nights, Santa's presents were hidden in a stocking by the open fireplace. The stocking often contained oranges and maybe even the odd apple and if they were really, really lucky, they might have some chocolate too!

Nowadays children have presents running into hundreds of pounds and in some cases, thousands of pounds. Such as state-of-the-art mobile phones, computers, etc. etc.

On this particular Christmas, should I have considered myself extremely fortunate to have a very big present indeed?

Well, the answer to that one is definitely a massive...

NO!!!

I wished I had never received it.

My present was the very last thing that I would have dreamed of or wanted to receive. Well, at least I shared it with the rest of Shropshire.

Because...

It was a Christmas hurricane!

You know, one of those big winds that blasts in excess of one hundred miles an hour.

Now, who in their right mind would want that for Christmas? I ask you?

Well certainly not me, especially with the pet hotel being full to the brim with cats and dogs.

In the early hours of Christmas morning, I lay in bed trying not to worry as the lashing rain and howling wind shook the windows of our cottage. We had experienced fierce winds before and fortunately; we were well sheltered on three sides by the bordering woodland. Even so, throughout that night I could not sleep and on numerous occasions got out of bed to look through the upstairs windows to make sure that the nearby cattery roof remained intact.

Or to be more precise...

Still there!

At Christmas time, Kathy and I started work one hour earlier at 7 a.m., even though it was still very dark. This enabled us to feed the cats before our staff arrived at 8 a.m.

We had fantastic staff, and on Christmas Days and Boxing Days they arrived spot on time whatever the weather wearing red and white Father Christmas hats. Now that is what you call a loyal workforce. I must add, that every year to show our appreciation, Kathy and I treated our manager and staff to a Christmas dinner and dance. This particular year we had a splendid time at the Victoria Hotel just down the road in Newport. With us so used to seeing our staff wearing wellies and waterproof clothing, we hardly recognised them as they danced the night away wearing their pretty dresses.

Christmas morning finally arrived and to my relief, the cattery building still had a roof. The wind was howling away, but not quite as bad as the previous night's rage. Unfortunately, it was still lashing down with bone-freezing rain.

In the cold winter's dawn, we greeted our well-wrapped merry workforce as they arrived on the car park. As you will have learned earlier, before they started the morning dog walking session, their first task was to shovel up the previous night's dog crap and empty the Muck Buckets into the septic tank.

However, my first task was to inspect every kennel block to make sure that they still had a roof.

The first two kennel blocks, kitchen, office buildings all proved to be intact and the dogs inside were as keen as ever to go out for their walks.

When I got to the third kennel block which was only six months old…

It was a different story…

To my horror, as I entered the kennel block the first two runs on the right that had a roof consisting of corrugated fibreglass sheets the evening before…

No longer had them!!!

'ARGHHH!!!'

The roofing sheets had been ripped off and were nowhere to be seen So, wherever those large roofing sheets eventually ended up was a mystery. I couldn't even hazard a guess on how many miles those airborne ten-foot-long sheets had achieved in the previous night's hurricane.

In the first run minus its roof stood a pair of long-haired German Shepherd dogs. The poor things were soaking wet and looked like miserable drowned rats. Why they hadn't had the good sense to retreat into their heated sleeping quarters where the roof was still intact, I will never know. Normally, German Shepherds are one of the most intelligent of breeds.

In the second run, although a little wet were two ordinary run-of-the-mill mongrel crosses. At least they had the good sense to retreat from the heavy pounding rain and shelter in their heated quarters.

Well, my Christmas Day working with the animals came to an abrupt end before it had ever started. Those four dogs needed rescuing by Geoff the maintenance man, dressed in his blue boiler suit and beige checkered cap.

Luckily, I still had some roofing sheets left over from previous work. Fortunately, as my nightmare Christmas Day progressed, the stiff wind subsided to a stiff breeze. If the hurricane had continued, it would have been impossible and downright dangerous for me to be handling those large light sheets on my own.

I could have ended up riding on a fibreglass sheet like Ali Baba on his magic carpet.

But with a much bumpier ride!

As I tackled my emergency roofing repairs, the German Shepherds were taken into our grooming room, where they were shampooed and dried with soothingly warm hair dryers to get their fluffy coats back to normal. By lunchtime, the German Shepherds were back in their run with new corrugated sheets bolted down, just as if nothing had ever happened.

I never informed their owners about their drenching, so, again, it was…

Thank Goodness They Can't Talk!

Well, that was one Christmas Day to remember, and I can definitely say I have had better.

Still, there was Boxing Day to look forward to...

Or was there?

I wish I hadn't said that because when Boxing Day dawned, we had an even bigger blow than the previous night.

'OH, NO! What am I going to find this time?'

Dozens of cats running all over the place crossed my mind.

Fortunately, it had nothing to do with cats. Thank goodness!

No, the latest damage had to do with people. To be exact, it concerned our staff.

Yes, our staff!

Because...

A large part of the staff room roof had gone walkabout. Or should I say, fly-about!

That was another load of roofing sheets that we were never going to see again. Unlike the fibreglass sheets, these sheets were much heavier because they were made from cementone a look-alike asbestos material. Let's just hope, that wherever those sheets ended up they had landed safely without taking somebody's head off!

To put a top hat on it, we also had a couple of sheets missing from the office roof as well.

I have to say, there wasn't too much good news flying around on that particular Boxing Day...

Did I say flying around?

At least it had stopped raining. Fortunately, I had similar sheets left over from previous building work to do that job as well.

The day after Boxing Day was a busy collection day and I was still working on the office roof, wearing my blue boiler suit and beige chequered cap.

At least it made me look the part.

As I worked, customers were entering the office eight feet below me. Cheerily I waved and wished them 'Merry Christmas'. They all waved back and returned my compliments.

All except one!

This lady arrived in her shiny Jaguar, sporting a personalised number plate. She was smartly dressed in designer gear and looked to be middle-aged. I waved and shouted 'Merry Christmas,' but there was no acknowledgement from her at all. She glared back up at me just as if I was something from beneath her shoe.

Maybe she thought I was just a cheeky workman. Anyway, she obviously didn't know who I really was. Meaning the VIP who happened to own the place!

It turned out that the lady in question had spoken to me on numerous occasions over the phone. Not only that. I was the only person she would talk to, not trusting anyone else to take a booking for her delightful cat, Primrose.

Coincidently, on a later occasion, we were expanding and I was bolting sheets on a new roof. I was getting along nicely when I was interrupted by Pat asking me to take a phone call. Reluctantly, I climbed down the ladder and followed Pat to the office.

As I entered the office, Pat covered the mouthpiece with her hand and whispered,

"You'll never guess who this is. She insists on only speaking to the nice Mr Doody to book her cat in."

Hey, guess who it was?

Can you believe?

It was the very same lady who would not say hello to me at Christmas when I was working on the office roof.

I wonder if Primrose's owner would have talked to me on the phone if she had known that I was wearing my blue boiler suit. If only I had known who it was the day after Boxing Day when she gave me that memorable discarding look. I would have climbed down and introduced myself.

Eventually, I met her when she brought Primrose in for another stay.

But I never did let on, that sometimes...

I was the maintenance hero, who wore a blue boiler suit and beige chequered cap!

CHAPTER 22

He's a Star!

This is where Kathy cannot see the wood for the trees.

Do you recognise the famous face in the caricature?

I find this short story about Kathy rather amusing.

Kathy has never had a good memory regarding people's faces as you will soon find out...

When Kathy worked for Barclays Bank, she was travelling back home from London on the train in a first-class carriage. For the whole journey she shared a carriage and sat opposite one of the most famous footballers of that era. It turned out to be John Barnes, who played for Liverpool and he was travelling with his daughter. In those days, Kathy was a keen Everton supporter and Liverpool were Everton's neighbours and bitter rivals. In other words, Kathy should have known who it was that she was chatting to. But she had no idea who they were.

Perhaps if John Barnes had hung his football boots around his neck, it might have given her a clue.

She never cottoned on why young boys and girls were continually walking past their carriage and shyly looking in at the chatting threesome.

Towards the end of the journey, some of the cheekier kids asked John Barnes for his autograph. It was only then that Kathy thought that this guy might be someone a little bit famous.

Perhaps John Barne's fans thought that he had acquired a secret girlfriend, meaning my attractive blonde-haired Kathy.

Kathy only found out who it was when she got home that night and explained to me what had happened on the train. I asked her to describe the person to me, and instantly, I knew who it was. So, a few years later, it was quite comical when a much more famous face was standing in front of Kathy in our office. He was a well-spoken gentleman who didn't know our area and was asking her for directions.

This particular gentleman was famous because he starred in the delightful TV series, All Creatures Great and Small. A well-loved situation comedy, drama, that has been adapted from the books by James Herriot.

So, have you guessed who it is from the caricature?

Well, it is the English actor Robert Hardy, who

played the role of Siegfried.

That evening, Robert Hardy was hosting an outdoor concert at Chetwynd Park just down the road from our premises. Kathy thought that she recognised his face and his very English accent did ring a bell, but she still could not place him. Well, she most certainly should have recognised him because it happened to be her favourite programme and she never missed one single episode!

I really wished that she had recognised him and called me because I would have been honoured to have had the chance to meet the great man.

There is one thing for certain, it would not be a very good idea for the police to ask Kathy to pick out a suspect in an identity parade!!!

CHAPTER 23

Famous Names and Look-alikes

More amusing stuff.

Two questions…

Do dog owners look like their dogs?

Do cat owners look like their cats?

Well, in my experience, having seen thousands of cats, dogs and customers, I cannot recall anybody resembling their cat.

With the vast amount of cats that boarded with us, we found that a lot of them came in pairs.

I don't think their owners actually thought that their cats looked like the famous names that they chose.

Well, I hope not!

Here are a few examples...

Botham and Brearley two famous cricketers. Perhaps their owners played cricket?

Arnie and Sevie two famous golfers. At least I knew that their owners played golf.

Morecambe and Wise two famous comedians. I don't know the answer to that one, but one of their owners did wear glasses. But that was the female side of the matrimonial partnership.

Charlie and Chaplin, the silent comedian from years ago. Both cats were black with white faces.

Rhubarb and Custard, their owners obviously liked this delicious English dessert.

Penny and Tuppence, two pre-decimalisation British coins. Perhaps their owners were quite old. I remember the cats, but not their owners.

Little and Large, two more famous comedians. One cat was small and the other was large.

Here are some more names that were given to cats and also dogs...

Abbott and Costello, Adam and Eve, Black and Decker, Fred and Ginger, Gin and Tonic, Howard and Hilda, Jack and Jill, Lennon and McCartney, Mork and Mindy, Romeo and Juliet, Salt and Pepper, Sonny and Cher, Sooty and Sweep, Tom and Jerry and last but not least Stan and Ollie.

Those are just to name a few. The list goes on and on.

As far as I am concerned, I do think certain people resemble their dogs.

I will guarantee that most of us when we think of Corgi's, will think of the late Queen of England. Now before I get sent to the Tower by King Charles, I would like to point out that from my point of view, the Queen looked nothing like a Corgi. Maybe Princess Margaret did?

Also, there was Queenie the Staffordshire Bull Terrier from the previous book. She had a lovely face, but definitely no resemblance to our late English Queen Elizabeth. And to make doubly sure, that I don't go to the Tower, I am very proud of King and country.

Going off on a tangent, as I often do, I think you are going to really like this one...

A shooting acquaintance of mine named John was a guest on a pheasant shoot at the magnificent Country Estate of Chatsworth House in Derbyshire. He was standing in the shooting line having shot several pheasants and waiting behind him to retrieve his downed pheasants was a petite lady wearing a tweed trilby hat and barber jacket. Accompanying her were two yellow Labrador Retrievers.

On a shoot, a person and their dog or dogs stand behind the shooting line of guns and they are known as 'Pickers up', a self-explanatory name. They pick up the shot pheasants or should I say the dogs under the guidance of the handler retrieve them. More often than not the dogs are directed into very dense thorny cover and it is a very skilful task.

Take note, John didn't know who this lady was as she stood patiently behind him.

He shouted to her,

"I HAVE THREE BIRDS DOWN IN THE BRACKEN ON THE LEFT AND FIVE IN THE BRIARS ON THE RIGHT."

Instantly, the good lady obeyed John and started working her two Labradors and it wasn't long before they found each bird. Carrying the dead birds by their necks, four in each hand, the lady handed them to John. As she did so, he almost fell backwards...

Because he had the shock of his life...

He almost had a coronary!

John realised that he had been giving orders to...

Her Majesty, Queen Elizabeth of England!!!

What about that for a story?

Okay, now back to the look-alikes.

The most common look-alike breeds seem to be Bulldogs. Did Sir Winston Churchill have one by any chance? All I know is a lot of Bulldog owners, didn't have squashed-up faces with wrinkles like their dogs, but they definitely had fat faces.

And the number of Bulldogs who were named Winston, or Churchill doesn't bear thinking about.

My father-in-law Ronnie, never owned a Bulldog, but there is no doubt about it, he featured one and he knew it too. He even sounded like the famous Bulldog named Churchill that advertised insurance on UK TV. Ronnie could take off the advert word for word and you would think that with his farming Cheshire accent, it really was the voice of the TV commercial's Bulldog.

Often, we had many a laugh in the office when an owner had either arrived or left with their look-alike dog.

Another customer who was waiting might say,

"Don't you think he resembles his dog?"

And he did!

The staff and I often noticed the likeness of dogs in comparison to their owner's faces.

When I think of all the breeds of dogs that there are. Which breed would anybody choose to look like if they had the choice?

HERE ARE A FEW...

Airedale, the owner could have short, tight curly hair.

To me, the Afghan Hound is quite a noble-looking dog. We had a lady customer who resembled her Afghan Hound. The lady in question was quite tall and slim with pointed features and long wavy blonde hair, a definite look-alike.

Do you think this photo of an Afghan Hound resembles a person?

Afghan Hound facts

The Afghan Hound is a majestic sight, with its long flowing hair and piercing eyes. Known for their independence, intelligence, and loyalty, they are a very old breed of dog and have a history dating back thousands of years. The Bedouin people of Afghanistan bred these dogs to hunt gazelle and other small game in the harsh terrain of the Afghan mountains. Afghan Hounds were not only used as war dogs by the Afghan army, but they were often depicted in historical art and literature. Today, they are still popular pets and are seen in dog shows and other competitions.

Then we had Poodles. A black Standard Poodle comes to my mind, he was called Mony. His owner had thick short black curly hair. Mony also reminded us of a friend of ours who is mentioned in some of my stories.

Here is the clue...

He is a close friend who has a career in law.

Yes, he is Mike our solicitor, Pepper's owner, the guy with a mouse in his hair!

Does this photo of a Standard Poodle look like anyone you know?

There were Basset Hounds, that have a mournful face.

We had a lady customer who looked just like her Basset Hound. Sorry Mam!

Bloodhounds, no we never had any of those, but the late Clement Freud comes to mind with his look-alike Bloodhound. In the 1960s, they became household names appearing in a series of TV commercials for dog food. Also, Quaker Oats (porridge) hired Clement Freud to appear with a Bloodhound named Henry (played by several dogs). The dogs shared his trademark 'hangdog' expression. It is not known if Clement Freud had his own canine companions.

The star of the Carry-On movies, the late, great Sid James springs to mind, he is a definite Bloodhound look-a-like.

Staffordshire Bull Terriers, their owners often looked quite macho, just like their dogs.

Then there were Labradors, Golden Retrievers, Jack Russells, Border Collies, West Highland Terriers and many, many more.

Then we come to my favourite dog, the Springer Spaniel. Do I look like one of them?

Nice dog anyway, who cares?

So the list could go on and on.

Yes, it is a fact that some people definitely do look a little like their dogs.

Can you think of any friends or people you know who resemble theirs?

As they say,

"The eye is in the beholder!"

Now, this leads me to the next caricature.

A Scottish one...

CHAPTER 24

Braveheart and his Filipino Takeaway

MICK

This is a mystery!

Yet another takeaway, this one is the third in this book series. This is another advert for readers who have not read the previous two books.

I had never heard of a Filipino takeaway until I met a certain Scottish gentleman.

The person concerned was certainly Scottish in his appearance and also his lingo. My problem was, I could not understand a word he was saying due to his very broad accent.

From his appearance, you would think he had arrived from centuries past. If he was given a kilt, claymore and shield, he could easily have gotten a part in the movie, Braveheart. He had a long straggly ginger beard and wore a red tartan Tam O'Shanter cap with a red pompom on the top. He almost looked like he was wearing a false beard and cap with red hair stuck out at the sides.

Tam O'Shanter caps are often worn by folks portraying comical Scotsmen in movies or on TV and very often spectators wear them at football and rugby matches.

But this guy was definitely for real and our staff nicknamed him Braveheart.

Braveheart wore glasses and I mean glasses. The lenses were so thick that they looked like bottle bottoms. They made his eyes look enormous. I could just imagine a young child looking into his magnified eyes and bursting into tears of fright.

Braveheart was one of our regular customers and

he always dressed in light brown tweedy clothes. He wore brown hobnail boots and the broad-toe caps shone so much that I could almost see my face in them. He had the appearance of a man from the mountains. Undoubtedly a Scottish Highlander. I must say, he was a very pleasant man whose noticeable appearance was a little unusual, to say the least. I was intrigued to know what his occupation was, but I was unable to hold a long enough conversation with him because of his indecipherable accent.

Braveheart owned five Border Collies, with biblical names, Matthew, Mark, Luke, John, and Peter.

And not a Sam amongst them!

Obviously, he was a religious man.

The Border Collies came with interesting leads. Baling twine! This made me think that they were from a farm. Perhaps he was a shepherd? Of course, when Braveheart left our premises we changed the bailing twine for standard leads.

Braveheart had been using our facilities for more than three years and on this particular day, his five Collies were dropped off in their usual tip-top condition. Their sleek coats were almost as shiny as their dad's toe caps. As Braveheart dropped them off, he informed me that he was off to the Philippines. Usually, he never said where he was going, that's if I managed to understand him. It was always simpler to wish him a good holiday rather than get into a long conversation. But, on this occasion, I became interested (or nosey) and managed to understand most of what he said.

I asked,

"I believe the Philippines is a nice place to go on holiday?"

"Och! I'm not going on holiday. I'm collecting a wife."

I looked at him in amazement and stuttered,

"Oh! How nice."

I was dumbfounded which is most unlike me.

I didn't blame him for going wife shopping, perhaps I am being a little unkind because I thought that he would never pull a lady in the UK with his rustic Highlander appearance even though he was a nice guy. I am sure he would have undoubtedly frightened off any females before he had a chance to chat them up with his indecipherable Highland twang.

'Good for you mate. I hope you come back with a Filipino beauty.'

In those days, buying Filipino girls for wives was common news, maybe even a fashion trend. I wasn't sure whether to believe him or not, but it looked very likely that we were going to find out the truth on our very own doorstep.

Braveheart was away for two weeks. Perhaps, included in the price was a honeymoon. Not a bad place to spend a honeymoon either. If they made each other happy, I could see nothing wrong with it.

That evening, I mentioned to Kathy what Braveheart was up to and said,

"If he comes back with a real cracker, you had better watch your step."

Without saying a word Kathy just gave me one of those looks that only your wife can give you!

'Time to shut up Geoff lad!'

Two weeks later, Braveheart returned and looked very triumphant with his spoils.

His bride most certainly was not the dolly bird that I had envisaged, but they looked very happy together, perhaps he thought he had got a bargain. Or had there been a sale in the Philippines?

Before Braveheart left our premises, he booked his Five Border Collies in again.

Four months later, Braveheart and his wife arrived on the car park and he was dressed in his usual attire, but strangely there were two Border Collies less. I wondered what could have happened to them. I didn't dare ask because I knew that he thought the world of them. Also, I couldn't spare the hour that I would have needed to decipher his dialect. The reason could have been something simple, such as a farmer friend taking care of them. Or even something tragic such as a road accident. But I did happen to notice when he and his new wife dropped off the three remaining Collies that they had put on considerable weight!

I mean the newlyweds, not the Collies!

I thought maybe his Filipino wife could have been pregnant.

But what about Braveheart?

Why had **HE** put on weight?

I have to admit, it crossed my mind...

'Do Filipino people eat dogs?'

But I had no intention of going down that road.

Two weeks passed by and the loving couple returned from their holiday looking very happy and relaxed as they collected the three remaining Border Collies. Before they left our premises they booked them in for another stay.

Three months later, Braveheart and his wife arrived on the given day, but wait for it...

Minus another Border Collie!

What on earth was happening to his dogs and where were the loving couple going every few months?

'How long would it have taken them to eat a Border Collie?'

My goodness, I didn't fancy hearing the answer!

Anyway, it is none of my business, so stop thinking about it Geoff lad.

After Braveheart and his Filipino wife collected their two surviving Border Collies, we never heard any more from them.

Were the surviving pair eaten?

We will never know!

Knowing that dogs are a delicacy in parts of Asia and noticing the loving couple had both put on weight!

I just hoped beyond hope, that I hadn't really witnessed a Filipino take-away....

Of the Border Collie variety!

CHAPTER 25

What a Terrible Smell!

A very pungent story!

Well, we have had a chapter about crap, now we have a chapter about pee. Cat pee to be precise! Do not worry this is only a short chapter.

Dog pee is quite a common smell and is quite pungent. Unfortunately, we often smell dog pee even if we don't own a dog because male dogs cock their legs up here, there and everywhere. The countless times I have cleaned my car and left it parked sparkling in the sun, only to come back later to find some dirty dog has cocked his leg and peed all over my lovely alloy wheels. Lamposts are a favourite peeing venue as well, but thankfully we don't have to clean them!

Have you ever heard the saying? 'As happy as a dog with twelve lampposts'!

Fox pee has a very strong scent and foxes use it to mark their territories like a lot of other animals. Horse pee smells strongly of ammonia, but you can put up with that as long as you do not take in too deep a breath. My personal view is that in the order of animal pee, our feline friends are pretty high up near the top of the list for being the most pungent. Most of us have smelt cat pee in our time, but this is usually from a neutered tom that has peed without permission in your beautiful flower bed. Cats are also attracted to catmint and that's why the little devils pee near it. Or on it!

Interesting facts about catmint

Catmint emits the odour of nepetalactone which triggers a kind of ecstasy in sexually mature cats. Nepetalactone is probably used by the plant has a natural defence against insects. This substance is very similar to the natural sex pheromones of cats. They get high on sniffing at catmint plants, roll on the floor and exhibit unusually playful behaviour. This would also explain why male cats in particular are so fond of catnip.

So, what are Pheromones?

You might be surprised to learn there are many different types of cat pheromones. The feline facial pheromone (FFP) is used when cats rub their faces on furniture and other objects. They're marking these with a pheromone that signals the objects are familiar and safe. The facial pheromones are produced by glands around the cat's cheeks and chin. Cats may bunt you with their heads to help put their scent on you and mark you as part of their colony. The cat-appeasing pheromone, in contrast, is used by a nursing mother cat to appease her newborn kittens helping to form a bond with her babies. Cat urine contains felinine, an amino acid with sulfur known as a putative pheromone precursor. This is especially prevalent in male cat urine and accounts for the odour. The scent works as a way of marking their territory. Cats also have a feline interdigital semiochemical produced by glands near their paws, helping mark their territory when they scratch or knead.

So, after reading that informative information, you must have learned something about cat habits, especially if you own or have owned one.

So, now it is back to good old cat pee...

Well, people think the smell of cat pee is pretty bad, but not too many individuals will have smelt the pee of an unneutered tom. This pure, unspoilt smell of pee is strongly advisable to be avoided at all costs. The smell of cat pee from a tom that has kept his testicles is probably ten times stronger than a tom that has had his surgically removed. Most owners of tom cats have them neutered when they are around six months old. Not only is this to stop the country from being overrun by hordes of cats, but it also helps to stop cats from spraying when they mark their territories.

The vile smell of an unneutered tom was the main reason we put on our cat booking forms.

IS YOUR CAT NEUTERED?

If the answer was no, our alarm bells started ringing. If a tom was in the region of six months old we insisted that it had to be neutered before it boarded with us.

Or it ain't coming in!!!

Any tom over that age would get an instant ban or the chop, not performed by me of course, but by a vet before it set foot on our premises.

I will now explain why.

In our early naive days, we had one or two toms that managed to slip through our net. Having experienced first-hand what it is like to look after an unneutered tom for a week, I can assure you, that it is a really bad experience which I don't want to repeat in my lifetime. It is not just the smell that is bad enough, but it is where the pee could end up that was our major concern.

For instance...

Would you believe?

Dripping off the ceiling!

Well, how does it get there?

You might well ask?

The answer is...

Because they spray it there.

That's how!

When a tom managed to penetrate our defences, it created havoc by virtually covering every inch of its accommodation with obnoxious stinking pee. They usually performed the filthy, foul deed during the night, totally ignoring the litter trays that we had provided.

Cats generally being clean creatures rarely urinated in their sleeping quarters.

Thank goodness for that!

When a tom who had retained his dangly bits had slipped through our net, we always knew we had made a major mistake well before we entered the cattery building.

Before we even set foot in the place, the foul smell whacked our nostrils.

When we worked in the cattery we wore rubber gloves, but if the stinking liquid did manage to get on our hands it could take hours of scrubbing or even days to rid our skin of the dreadful pungent smell. If I was unfortunate enough to acquire the smell of tom pee on my hands I made doubly sure that I avoided food that required using my hands, such as sandwiches.

For sure, eating sandwiches wearing rubber gloves did not appeal to my appetite!

In the early days of running the pet hotel when I worked alone, I had the unavoidable responsibility of looking after one of those toms with testicles.

The vile problem caused me to lie awake during the night worrying...

'*What sight or smell is going to greet me in the morning*?'

Once we had made the awful mistake of accepting a tom with his dangly bits, there was no way of getting rid of it until his owner collected him. I must admit, I was more than tempted to throw it out into the woodland where it would have been able to pee to its heart's content.

Now I am sure you realise our reason for that very important question on the cat booking forms.

IS YOUR CAT NEUTERED?

CHAPTER 26

The Escape Artist

MICK

Thomas is the cat that gave us the biggest problem ever!!!

Kathy did not want me to write this story because she thought it could be detrimental to our past reputation. But this is another true story that has to be told. Yet another one of my secrets revealed.

After all my security involving the cattery building, this was definitely, 'A Cat on the Run'.

This particular Saturday was as good as it gets for mowing grass. As we all know in the UK, fitting grass mowing between showers in the wet summers that we endure can be a nightmare.

And this day turned into a...

NIGHTMARE!!!

Mowing the grass turned out to be one of my biggest and most enjoyable tasks. I always tried to cut all of it on the same day which included the large lawn between the cattery and kennel buildings and also the lawns in our garden. As I sat on my little red tractor mower this satisfying task took me just under four hours.

And that was if I had no interruptions!

On this particular day, there was a very upsetting interruption!!!

I had been on the tractor for about an hour reflecting how good life was as I admired my magnificent friends the swallows whizzing by feeding on the insects that my grass cutting had disturbed. I was my own boss. Or should I say? I was when Kathy was not around. Although I did get more than enough stick from my manager Pat at times. The business was booming and I am quite proud to say that we had become one of the most popular pet hotels in mid-England.

On that dreamy tranquil morning as I sat nonchalantly on my mower, life was really, really good, but as usual, it did not last for long...

I have lost count of the number of times that I have heard someone shouting,

"GEOFF! GEOFF! COME QUICK!"

Little did I know, that today was going to be no exception...

I was mowing by the car park and U-turned the tractor to make my way back down the straight line of grass I had cut towards the cattery. I was about halfway down when I noticed Ann. She was looking more than a little bit impatient. She was gesticulating, obviously in a bid to get me to hurry up.

Even though I was wearing ear defenders I could faintly hear that well-used name,

"GEOFF! GEOFF!"

I was in second gear because the grass was too thick for me to put the tractor in third and I knew that I would be with Ann in less than half a minute.

But the closer I got, the more impatient she was getting.

'What on earth is the matter with her? I've seen it all before. You'll just have to wait until I get to you. It can't be that important!'

The more I closed the gap, the more it dawned on me that my fantastic day was coming to an abrupt end.

I felt like turning my red machine around and disappearing over the green horizon.

Eventually, when I got to her, I could see by the expression on her face that she was completely distressed.

I killed the engine, removed my ear defenders and asked,

“Whatever is the matter?”

“We’ve lost a cat!”

“What do you mean? We’ve lost a cat?”

Ann's voice rose to a stressed-out crescendo,

“GEOFF! AREN’T YOU LISTENING? WE HAVE LOST A CAT!!!”

“How can we lose a cat with all the security we have?”

Ann was quite tearful, in fact bordering on hysterical as she replied,

"I'm telling you Geoff we've lost a cat. It's definitely gone, almost like it's vanished into thin air."

"Okay. Calm down. Tell me what happened?"

"He's gone. There is just no sign of him anywhere. The cat that was with him is still in the run. But he's gone!"

"What do you mean he's gone? Gone where? How's he got out and why is the other one still there if he's gone?"

"Geoff! Will you just stop asking me stupid questions and come and take a look for yourself!"

Apprehensively, I followed her into the cattery building and walked down to where the missing cat should be.

To my absolute horror...

ANN WAS RIGHT!!!

The cat had gone!

Ann added,

"He was here when I fed them both this morning and when I came back to check his bedding, there was no sign of him. He has just disappeared into thin air."

"Have you checked the other runs? He could be hiding in one of the empty ones?"

"I'm not stupid. I have checked absolutely everywhere. And that cat is not in this cattery."

"OH NO! When is he due to be collected by the owners?"

Now, that is when the really bad news came.

Ann answered,

"This afternoon."

I yelled,

"OH, NO!"

Then Ann asked the million-dollar question,

"How are we going to find him before they get here?"

That was the million-dollar question that I had no answer to.

The missing cat's name was Thomas and all we

could do was search for him, but where should we start?

How long had he been gone?

How far could he have strayed?

How long is a piece of string?

Ann had seen Thomas less than two hours ago, but that meant nothing, especially with him having a two-hour start. He could be anywhere!!!

Along with the staff that we could spare, we searched high and low for Thomas for more than three hours. Searching for a small cat in one hundred acres of surrounding woodland was like looking for a needle in the proverbial haystack. Unfortunately for us and of course Thomas, there was no sign of him. I was the one who was going to have to face the music and break the terrible news to his owners. What made it even worse and personal, they had been recommended by my sister Gail.

So much for the perks of running a first-class pet-boarding establishment!

When his owners Mr and Mrs Plant arrived, (false names) I tried to explain in the calmest possible way that unfortunately, we had lost Thomas. As you can imagine, they were far from happy. The only consolation I could offer was, at least we still had the other one.

Mr Plant's face was as white as a sheet and I could see that he was shaking as he tried to control his temper. His wife was crying, their two children were crying, Ann was crying, and I wanted to cry too.

But where was that going to get me?

'Oh my! If only, the Plant's had collected their cats yesterday or even first thing this morning when Ann had fed them.'

Mr Plant looked at me savagely, almost as if I had lost his cat on purpose. I could tell by the look on his face that he felt like breaking my neck. And probably would have if he hadn't been a friend of my sister!

And who could blame him?

With every defensive word I uttered, it just made things worse and I seemed to be digging a hole for myself that was getting deeper and deeper by the second. I felt as if I was falling into a bottomless pit. At that moment, I wished I could have disappeared into that bottomless pit.

In a seething temper through clenched teeth, he said,

“When we dropped him off, I told you that he was an escape artist and he hates being touched.”

I had no choice, but to grovel,

“I am really, really sorry. We just don’t know how he’s got out.”

He snarled and spoke through gritted teeth,

“Well has! Hasn’t he?”

“Yes, I am afraid he has.”

“Well, what are you going to do about it?”

“Everything we possibly can.”

“Well, what is that supposed to mean?

“I don’t know.”

He yelled,

"WELL, YOU HAD BETTER FIND OUT!”

Thomas's owner had totally lost it, he was shaking and his face was whiter than white. I could not say or do any more that would have helped the ugly situation. I decided to take the distressed family down to the cattery and show them where Thomas had lived for the last two weeks.

After inspecting our security in the inside and outside of the cattery building, reluctantly they agreed that Thomas had done the impossible!

He had escaped!!!

But how?

None of us could fathom out how. Even if he had escaped out of his run, he would have had to pass through two more spring-loaded security doors without any of the staff noticing.

Stupidly, I said,

"I told you that this place is like Fort Knox."

He turned white-faced and looked at me very aggressively,

"If you don't shut up, I'll shut you up!"

I decided if I wanted to see tomorrow in one piece, now was the time to keep as quiet as possible.

Ann, Kathy and me, along with numerous members of staff, including the escaped cat's family spent the following two hours walking through the one hundred acres of woodland searching and calling Thomas's name.

Sadly, to no avail!

Unfortunately, there was no happy ending to this sad story. Thomas had escaped and was never to be seen again. So, that was it!

My burning question was...

How on earth could he have possibly escaped?

I just had to find out. It was a real worry because if one cat could get out then others could follow. I trusted my staff implicitly and I knew if they had seen Thomas slip by as they were cleaning they would have informed me. Therefore, I concluded that there must be an escape route from his run.

I was determined to find out exactly where. And how?

I went into Thomas's run but I just could not see any obvious way out...

It was almost as if he had passed through the solid wall or the corrugated fibreglass roof.

The thing is, how could I advertise our cattery as being the most secure in the Midlands if there was a secret way out? If I was unable to find Thomas's secret escape route, then an army of cats could use it. (Slight exaggeration.)

But why hadn't Thomas's companion followed him out that morning?

There had to be a solution and I was determined to solve it. But the more I searched, the more puzzled I became. I scrutinised all sorts of angles from within Thomas's vacant run and the rest of the cattery building.

There was just no way a cat could escape!

I fetched a ladder from our garage and climbed up onto the cattery roof to check it out. With the roof consisting of corrugated fibreglass sheets, I had to be very careful where I walked so I only stepped on the places that were bolted to the wooden joists to make sure that I did not damage the roof or even fall through it.

Gingerly, I made my way towards Thomas's run, checking the lines of brass bolts above each run that I had meticulously bolted down myself. Also, when I originally fixed the fibreglass sheets to the wooden joists, I made doubly sure that there was a bolt fixed through every raised contour of the corrugation. Every other one would have been sufficient, but I had taken no chance at all and secured every last one. A cat should not have had 'A cat in hell's chance' of escaping through that roof because every bolt seemed intact and none were missing.

So, how had Thomas done it?

I was baffled!

I knelt down above Thomas's run and inspected each bolt by feeling them to make sure that they hadn't worked loose...

To my disbelief...

One moved!!!

'OH NO!'

'This is impossible. How can it be loose?'

The brass bolts were four inches long, screwed deeply into wooden joists and it would have been impossible for a man to loosen one of those bolts even with a claw hammer, let alone a small cat with claws.

But the one above Thomas's run was definitely loose.

I pulled at the corrugated sheet and it lifted slightly.

It had to be his escape route.

In my determination to solve the distressing riddle, I shot back down the ladder and ran around the back of the cattery to Thomas's run. I pushed the corrugated sheet in question upwards which took quite a bit of effort and I managed to create a gap that was no more than three inches wide by three inches high.

I scrutinised the gap very closely to see if there was any cat hair attached to the end of the corrugated sheet...

AND THERE WAS THE CLUE!

There were a couple of hairs clinging to the end

of the corrugated sheet.

Exactly, the same colour as Thomas's.

Riddle solved!

That was no consolation for me having lost a well-loved family cat. I pledged to myself there and then...

No other cat was ever going to escape from my cattery again...

I hurried back up onto the roof and checked and double-checked every single bolt. Thankfully, no more bolts were the slightest bit loose. The bolt above Thomas's run was the only one, and he had found it. But why? I was puzzled. Why was this the only loose bolt out of hundreds? Coincidentally, why did it have to be the bolt above his run? The little devil must have loosened the bolt by continually pushing and pressing his head against the corrugated sheet.

I went into Thomas's run and yet I looked up…

To my horror, that is when I spotted what had caused the distressing problem…

The brass bolt was screwed into a big knot that

had dried out and cracked slightly.

'ARGHHH!!!'

So, why did it have to be Thomas who found that loose knot?

What an incredible, but terrible coincidence!

Thomas must have been very determined to escape by working so hard in that weakened area. We were just so unlucky that he had managed to achieve his aim and squeeze through the tiny gap which he had created.

Especially on the morning of his departure!

'ARGHHH!!!'

If you could have seen the minute gap that Thomas had managed to squeeze through, you would never have believed it. And he was a full-grown cat. Not a kitten!

How knots form in wood

As a tree grows, its trunk increases in width. Soon, the trunk grows much larger than the branches that grow out of it. It is common to see knots emerging from around the branches of these trees and thickening in size as the tree keeps on growing. As the branches of the tree continue to grow, they are quickly overtaken by the tree trunk where a solid knot forms and contains live wood. The knot comprises very thick and tough wood, much more than the wood surrounding it and may end up as a big bulge around a branch that spouts from its middle. A loose knot forms when a branch is injured or dies when it is still part of the tree. The tree trunk continues to grow larger naturally. These kinds of knots are very much like tight knots, except that at their core they do not have living wood, but dead or rotting wood material. This matter lying at the heart of the knot is loosely structured and easily removable, often causing an empty vacuum to remain like a hole in the tree trunk, amidst sturdy trunk wood.

I will never fix a screw or a bolt in knotty wood again. As they say, 'You live and learn.'

After that awful disaster, I stepped up our security even more and fixed lengths of galvanised metal straps across all the corrugated sheets. I completed the task in record time, which made the cattery roof absolutely escape-proof. And as a bonus, totally windproof.

After that added security, no other cat managed to escape from our cattery again.

I believe that Thomas was a cat in a million. Only he could have achieved this amazing feat and to this very day, I still feel very sorry towards his owners. I also think that I was very lucky on that Saturday that I wasn't set upon by Mr Plant who I am sure wanted to kill me in his seething temper. And I don't blame him either. I would have felt exactly the same if the roles had been reversed and it had been my cat.

It was a pure miracle that their cat had managed to do a runner and no one was really to blame except that escape artist...

Thomas!

The strange thing was, he had eaten well, which meant that he had not been under any stress in any way at all. The girls had even managed to pick him up and cuddle him, unlike the advice given by his owners that he did not like being touched.

I only hope that Thomas found what he was looking for out there in the wild woodland. I am sure he would not have starved, especially with the amount of birds, mice and rabbits that inhabited the area. It is a fact that if a roaming cat is hungry it soon turns wild and becomes a proficient hunter. All cats have a natural instinct and ability to hunt and eventually will turn feral.

Hopefully, by telling this story, I have proven that it should not be detrimental to our past reputation which by the way we are still very proud of.

At the end of the day, all I can say is that was a very traumatic experience.

So, it's bye, bye Thomas and hello to Bruno and Lady in the next exciting story.

CHAPTER 27

Bruno Gets His Just Deserves

Nearly a bite in the tail!

Bruno is the Doberman that I read a postcard to in the first book of this series when a group of disbelieving customers thought that I was crazy!

Unfortunately, as nice as he was, Bruno had a very nasty habit of aggressively lunging at other dogs during our dog-walking sessions.

And it was infuriating!

Bruno the bully only picked on the much smaller breeds and frightened the living daylights out of them. He never seemed to attack anything approaching the size of a Labrador. So, in sheer fright, the small dogs cowered away from his bullying lunges. But the tiny Jack Russells who are fearless lunged straight back at big Bruno winding him up even more.

Well, as far as small dogs are concerned Bruno was a bully, but thank goodness he loved people.

Especially us!

During one of Bruno's stays, we had a lovable St. Bernard boarding at the same time and her name was Lady. As most people know the St. Bernard breed is big and when I say big, I mean big. And Lady was no exception! In fact, she was massive, almost the size of a small donkey. Despite her size, Lady was a gentle giant with all forms of life on the planet. She had never shown any sign of aggression in any shape or form to man or beast. She was completely the opposite to Bruno and loved the miniature breeds. Therefore, on our woodland circuit to save time she was always walked with one miniature and sometimes two.

Facts about the St. Bernard breed

The St. Bernard is a breed of very large working dog from the western Alps in Italy and Switzerland. They were originally bred for rescue by the hospice of the Great St. Bernard Pass on the Italian-Swiss border. The hospice built by and named after Italian monk Bernard of Menthon, acquired its first dogs between 1660 and 1670. The breed has become famous through tales of alpine rescues, as well as for its enormous size.

The giant St. Bernard weighs between 140 to 260 lbs (65 to 120 kg) or more, and the approximate height at the withers is 28 to 35 ins (70 to 90 cm). The coat can be either smooth or rough. The smooth coat is close and flat, while the rough is dense, flat and more profuse around the neck and legs. The colour is typically a red shade with white or a mahogany brindle with white. Black shading is usually found on the face and ears. The tail is long and heavy, hanging low. Eyes are usually brown, but sometimes can be icy blue and should have naturally tight lids, with the membrane only slightly visible. St. Bernards are often portrayed, especially in old live action comedies such as Swiss Miss, the TV series Topper, and classic cartoons, wearing small barrels of brandy around their necks. Avalanche victims supposedly drank the brandy to stay warm when awaiting rescue, although this is medically unsound.

One afternoon, I was walking Lady with Lucy a white Miniature Poodle and one of our girls Charlotte was walking Bruno.

Unavoidably, our paths crossed...

Creating instant mayhem!

Big Bruno lunged violently at Lucy...

The normally placid St. Bernard went from standstill to guided missile speed...

STRAIGHT AT BRUNO!!!

In desperation, I was doing my utmost best to hang onto Lady by digging my heels as I tried to avoid the oncoming onslaught. On seeing the frightening sight of a seething St. Bernard in full screaming battle cry charging right at him, Bruno in severe shock almost disappeared...

Up his own backside!!!

Bruno spun Charlotte around in the opposite direction and her feet were hardly touching the ground as she tried to cope with Bruno's fleeing attempt to reach the sanctuary of his sleeping quarters with the charging monster right on his tail. In the heat of the moment, the kennel proprietor, meaning me, was desperately hanging on to the infuriated St. Bernard and had no choice but to drag the terrified Poodle with me. For sure, I would have had more control if I had saddled Lady up and rode on her back!

Well, the good news for the cowardly Bruno was, he made it back to safety with all his bits intact.

But only just!

I don't know why the gentle St. Bernard attacked him, but more than likely she did not like his ungentlemanly bullying behaviour towards her tiny friend Lucy.

After Bruno's terrifying ordeal with a seething giant of a dog much bigger than himself, it must have taught the subdued bully a lesson that he wouldn't forget because he never made another attack on any of our miniature canine guests again.

And he sure didn't attack a big one either!

All thanks to the gentle giant of a St. Bernard, our Lady who certainly put him in his place.

CHAPTER 28

My second incredible encounter with nature

This final story takes place in the Kingdom of Thailand and it is all about being in the right place at the right time just as I was with the female Woodcock in the previous book of this series.

Kathy and I now live in Thailand and because we are getting on a bit in years the warm weather is more inviting than the inclement weather of the UK. Here we are able to keep fit by swimming every day and cycling on mountain bikes three times a week. Another reason we live here along with other numerous expats is that it is far more affordable than our homeland of Britain which we still love.

This adventure happened when we were out cycling. We weren't on a mountainous dirt track, (and there are many) but on a quiet tarmac road in an unpopulated area very close to a golf course. For us, one of the main attractions of cycling in Thailand is that we encounter various forms of wildlife. Such as exotic birds, snakes and quite frequently very large monitor lizards.

Here are a few examples...

A stunning bee-eater

A hoopoe, a bird that occasionally visits Britain

A sunbird another stunner

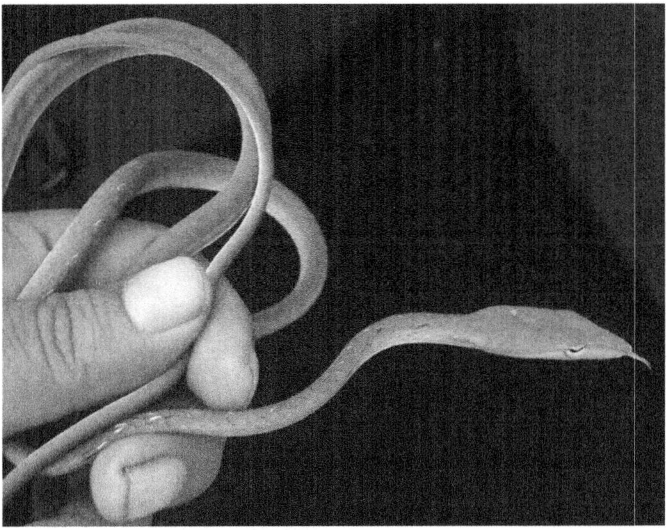

A beautiful harmless slender vine snake

A giant monitor lizard

This massive lizard, which is protected in

Thailand, can grow to more than 6 ft (2 mt) in length. Monitor lizards are the most intelligent of all lizards and have forked tongues like snakes, which they use to detect prey scents in the air and are excellent swimmers. Generally, when we are cycling we see them crossing a road or swimming in a quiet pond or lake. One memorable day in our garden, we observed a monitor lizard that was climbing to the top of a coconut tree more than a hundred feet off the ground in a bid to rob a hoopoe's nest from a hole at the top. Mobbed by the distressed hoopoes it gave up and shinned down the tree backwards. Kathy and I did not realise that a large creature such as a monitor lizard was capable of climbing so high and we were amazed by its determination.

And now here is our wondrous encounter with one of Thailand's rarest animals...

Starting from our home that has a woodland/ jungle view, we are very lucky to have several cycle rides to choose from. On this particular day, we chose a route that we call the Bougainvillea Ride. This route takes us past the entrance of Siam Golf Course. We had just completed a long uphill stretch of tarmac taking us to a right turn that led to a quiet road that has a central reservation of multi-coloured bougainvillea. (Hence the name that we had come up with.) I was leading and we had cycled about forty yards when it happened...

A strange-looking dog was staring straight at us as it nonchalantly trotted from left to right across the road only thirty yards in front of us.

Kathy was right behind me, I stopped pedalling and in my amazement I shouted as quietly as I could,

"KATH! QUICK! LOOK AT THAT! IT LOOKS LIKE A FOX."

I knew that there were no foxes in Thailand and reached for my phone to take a photo, but it took too long for me to get it out of the bag on the front of the bike. By that time, the unusual fox-looking creature was disappearing into the dense cover on the other side of the road.

I said to Kathy,

"I have never seen an animal like that before. It looked half fox. I am sure it is some kind of wild dog."

Kathy said,

"It had a fox's face as it looked directly at us."

I replied,

"Yes, it has and did you see the shape of its bushy tail?

I added,

"I have seen loads of foxes in my time, but I have never seen one looking like that."

I was curious to see where it had gone, so I rode diagonally across the road followed by Kathy to the spot where it had vanished and we both dismounted.

Excitedly, I pointed to the ground and said,

"Look there are prints here! This is a well-worn path, there must be more of these fox-looking creatures using it."

I turned and looked across the other side of the road then said,

"Look! There's a gap in the hedge. They must be using this track on a regular basis. When we get back I will check on the computer for wild dogs in Thailand and see what comes up."

We were quite excited about our morning's amazing encounter with nature and could not wait to get home to satisfy our curiosity. So, that is what we did and when we researched it we found out just how lucky we were...

Amazingly, at close range, we had observed a Dhole, a very rare Asian wild dog. I took a photo off the computer and showed it to numerous Thai acquaintances. Many said that they had seen Dholes on TV nature programmes, but never in the wild. Indeed, we have been very lucky because we have been back there many, many times since to try and catch another glimpse of this very rare wild dog, the Dhole, but to no avail.

Facts about Dholes

Dholes are listed as endangered as the populations throughout Asia are decreasing and are estimated at 949 to 2,500 adults. Factors contributing to this decline include habitat loss, loss of prey, competition with other species, persecution, and disease transfer from domestic dogs. The Dhole is a highly social animal, living in large clans without rigid dominance hierarchies and containing multiple breeding females. Such clans usually consist of 12 individuals, but groups of over 40 are known. Dholes produce loud whistles resembling the calls of red foxes. The Dhole is a diurnal pack hunter which preferentially targets medium and large-sized prey in tropical forests. Dholes compete with tigers and leopards targeting somewhat different prey species, but still with substantial dietary overlap. In appearance, the Dhole has been described as combining the physical characteristics of the grey wolf and red fox and being 'cat-like' on account of its long backbone and slender limbs. Adults may weigh over 40 lb (18 kg) with females usually weighing 9.9 lb (4.5 kg) a lot less than males. It stands 17–22 inches (43.18 cm - 55.88 cm) at the shoulder and measures 3 ft (almost 1 mt) in body length. Like the African Wild Dog, its ears are rounded rather than pointed.

After those enlightening facts about Dholes, I do hope you have enjoyed this book series as much as I have enjoyed writing it.

After reading about our adventures, some of them traumatic. This is a question you might like to ask me,

"If you had your life again, would you open another pet hotel?"

And my answer is,

"Of course, I would. I would not miss it for the

world!!!”

My question to you is,

“Would you?”

ACKNOWLEDGEMENT

To my incredible wife Kathy, who has had the patience of a saint to work with me over the years that it has taken me to write and publish this three-book series. She painstakingly typed my awful long hand and helped me revamp it hundreds of times into this collection of stories.

My sincere thanks to Mick who has drawn the outstanding detailed caricatures, giving the book its very own personality.

I would like to thank all my family, friends, and customers. And of course, not forgetting the main characters, the cats and dogs who created the stories.

A special thanks to my managers, Clare, Debbie, Kick, Pat and Erica.

And to all my girls, Tracey, Haley, Jenny, Gill,

Hannah, Caroline, Charlotte, Amy and any other staff that I might have inadvertently left out.

Although all the stories are based on true facts, some names have been changed to protect identities.

AUTHOR BIO

Geoff was born in Newport, a small historic market town in the county of Shropshire, England. Here, he was involved in various businesses. His diversified career ranged from, shopkeeper, restauranter, sales rep, gamekeeper, builder. And finally, the pet hotel that inspired Geoff's very funny autobiographical stories in this three-book series.

The pet hotel known as Chetwynd Firs, is still situated in an idyllic spot north of Newport, off the A41 highway. Newport is very close to the Staffordshire border; therefore, the business served those two counties, plus Cheshire and a large part of the Midlands.

Geoff and Kathy live in Thailand with three cats, Drambuie, Sambuca and Tia Maria.

Printed in Great Britain
by Amazon

36678925R00255